1001 WINNING
CHESS SACRIFICES
AND COMBINATIONS

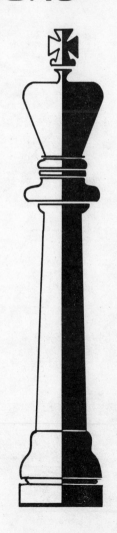

ABOUT THE AUTHOR

Howard Simon

FRED REINFELD is a native New Yorker. It was in the city schools and at City College that he began his chess-playing. While still in his teens he became Intercollegiate Champion, and was victorious in the New York State, Manhattan Club and Marshall Club Championship matches, beating such worthy opponents as Sammy Reshevsky, Reuben Fine, Arnold Denker and Al Horowitz.

Mr. Reinfeld has been one of the editors of "Chess Review" since its start in 1933. He is a prolific writer, with more than 50 chess books to his credit. On the staff of New York University, he teaches chess to hundreds of students yearly.

1001 WINNING CHESS SACRIFICES AND COMBINATIONS

by

FRED REINFELD

1973 EDITION

Published by

WILSHIRE BOOK COMPANY

12015 Sherman Road

No. Hollywood, California 91605

Telephone: (213) 875-1711

OTHER BOOKS BY FRED REINFELD

Third Printing

Copyright, 1955
by Sterling Publishing Co., Inc.

All rights reserved under International and
Pan-American Copyright Conventions

Manufactured in the United States of America

Library of Congress Card No. 55-7430

Printed by
HAL LEIGHTON PRINTING CO.
P. O. Box 1231
Beverly Hills, California 90213
Telephone: (213) 346-8500

Table of Contents

Chess Notation 10

Introduction—Sacrifices and Combinations 11

1. Pinning 12

2. Knight Forks 31

3. Double Attack 44

4. Discovered Attack 64

5. Discovered Check 74

6. Double Check 83

7. The Overworked Piece 88

8. Removing the Guard 98

9. Clearance 111

10. Interference 118

11. Queening Combinations 126

12. The Vulnerable First Rank 134

13. Queen Sacrifices 141

14. X-ray Attack 151

15. Surprise Moves 156

16. Defensive Combinations 163

17. Trapped Man 169

18. Zugzwang 172

19. The Helpless King 175

20. The Weakened Castled Position 182

21. Solutions 199

CHESS NOTATION

As indicated in the following diagram, all the squares on the chessboard are *numbered* from both sides of the board; White's KR1, for example, is Black's KR8. Each square is also *named* for the piece occupying the file. Below the diagram is a list of the chief abbreviations used in chess notation.

BLACK

QR1 / QR8	QN1 / QN8	QB1 / QB8	Q1 / Q8	K1 / K8	KB1 / KB8	KN1 / KN8	KR1 / KR8
QR2 / QR7	QN2 / QN7	QB2 / QB7	Q2 / Q7	K2 / K7	KB2 / KB7	KN2 / KN7	KR2 / KR7
QR3 / QR6	QN3 / QN6	QB3 / QB6	Q3 / Q6	K3 / K6	KB3 / KB6	KN3 / KN6	KR3 / KR6
QR4 / QR5	QN4 / QN5	QB4 / QB5	Q4 / Q5	K4 / K5	KB4 / KB5	KN4 / KN5	KR4 / KR5
QR5 / QR4	QN5 / QN4	QB5 / QB4	Q5 / Q4	K5 / K4	KB5 / KB4	KN5 / KN4	KR5 / KR4
QR6 / QR3	QN6 / QN3	QB6 / QB3	Q6 / Q3	K6 / K3	KB6 / KB3	KN6 / KN3	KR6 / KR3
QR7 / QR2	QN7 / QN2	QB7 / QB2	Q7 / Q2	K7 / K2	KB7 / KB2	KN7 / KN2	KR7 / KR2
QR8 / QR1	QN8 / QN1	QB8 / QB1	Q8 / Q1	K8 / K1	KB8 / KB1	KN8 / KN1	KR8 / KR1

WHITE

King — K	check — ch	
Queen — Q	discovered check — dis ch	
Rook — R	double check — dbl ch	
Bishop — B	en passant — e.p.	
Knight — N	good move — !	
Pawn — P	very good move — ! !	
captures — x	outstanding move — ! ! !	
to — —	bad move — ?	

Sacrifices and Combinations

The man who wrote, "Tactics is 99 per cent of chess," might well have added—"and 99 per cent of the fun, too!"

Brilliant sacrifices and combinations, either calculated in advance or played on the spur of the moment, give us thrills that cannot be equaled by any other aspect of the game. And, by a very fortunate coincidence, these brilliant strokes are just what we need in order to become first-rate players.

But then comes the practical question: How do we learn to become brilliant players? (Or is this a knack that one has to be born with?) The answer is reassuring: *Every chessplayer, no matter what his degree of skill may be, can learn how to play brilliant chess.*

The first step toward mastery is to become familiar with the different types of tactical motifs. The second step is to study a great many examples of these tactical themes. So, the object of this book is to add to your knowledge, to make you a strong chessplayer, and (last but not least) to delight you with some of the most beautiful moves ever played on the chessboard.

I. Pinning

The pin is by far the most frequently used tactical theme. It may be defined as *an attack on a piece which screens a second piece from attack.* The unit attacked in this way is said to be pinned. If attacked with enough force and ingenuity, it can often be won or completely disabled. Some examples:

In Diagram 2 Black's Knight is subject to an "absolute" pin. (This is the term we use when the King is the screened piece.) Worse yet, the Knight is pinned in two ways, by the White Queen and Bishop. And still worse, the Knight is not protected by a Pawn, which is the best—and cheapest—defense for a pinned piece. All these weaknesses combine to make possible White's brilliant demolition of Black's position.

In Diagram 5 we see again the fatal effect of an "absolute" pin. Once we're familiar with the pinning motif, we become used to the idea of *creating* pins—as for example in Diagram 16, where White first sacrifices in order to win Black's Queen by means of a pin.

Sometimes a pin defeats an already existing pin. Diagram 11 is a thrilling example of this.

A frequent use of the pin is to "pile up" on the pinned piece with an effective Pawn advance, as in Diagram 17. The piling-up may also be performed by pieces—sometimes with startling effect, as in Diagram 1.

WHITE MOVES FIRST

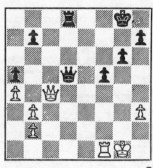

1

2

3

4

5

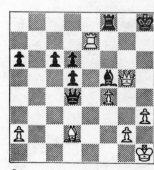

6

WHITE MOVES FIRST

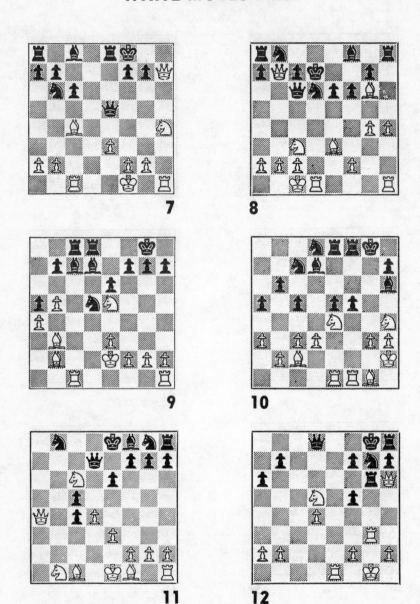

7

8

9

10

11

12

14 · PINNING ·

WHITE MOVES FIRST

13

14

15

16

17

18

WHITE MOVES FIRST

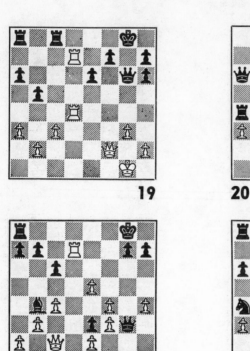

19

20

21

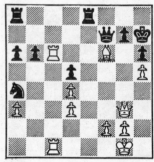

22

23

24

16 · PINNING ·

WHITE MOVES FIRST

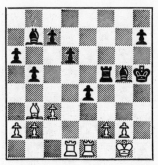

25

26

27

28

29

30

WHITE MOVES FIRST

31

32

33

34

35

36

18 · PINNING ·

WHITE MOVES FIRST

37

38

39

40

41

42

WHITE MOVES FIRST

43

44

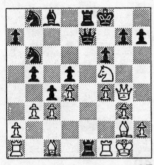

45

46

47

48

20 · PINNING ·

49

50

51

52

53

54

WHITE MOVES FIRST

55

56

57

58

59

60

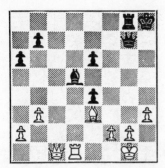

61

62

63

64

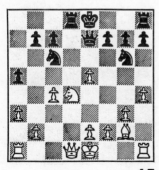

65

66

WHITE MOVES FIRST

67

68

69

70

71

72

BLACK MOVES FIRST

73

74

75

76

77

78

79

80

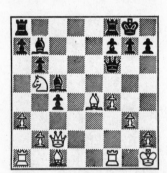

81

82

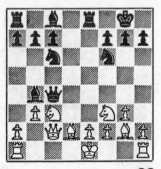

83

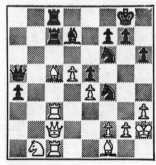

84

BLACK MOVES FIRST

85

86

87

88

89

90

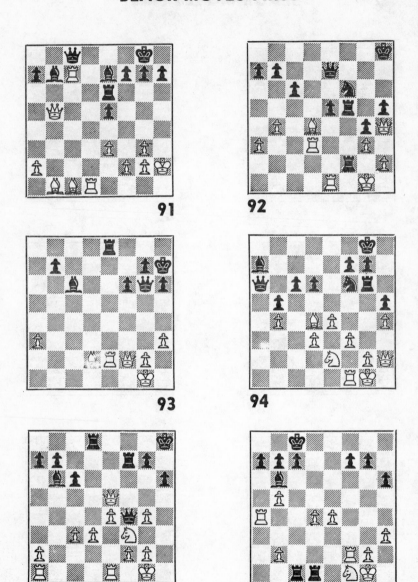

91

92

93

94

95

96

BLACK MOVES FIRST

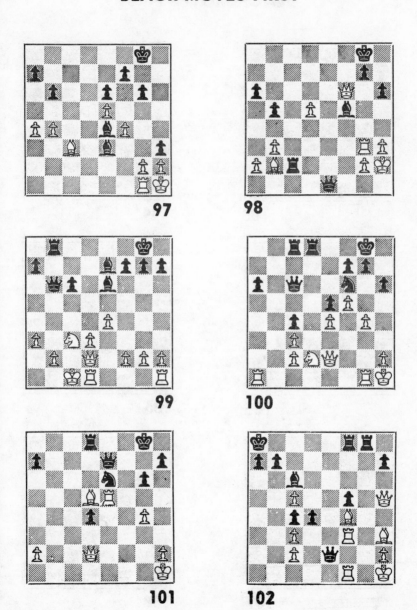

97

98

99

100

101

102

BLACK MOVES FIRST

103

104

105

106

107

108

30 · PINNING ·

2. Knight Forks

The Knight fork is the most popular tactical theme aside from the pin. Actually, the Knight fork is a special case of the double attack—*an attack on two units by a single unit*. But the Knight fork is particularly effective, and particularly dreaded, especially by inexperienced players.

Sometimes the Knight fork appears in a fairly simple setting, as in Diagram 112, where it is merely necessary to give a Knight check as a preliminary to the winning fork.

In some cases a more or less subtle preliminary is needed to set the stage for the fork. Diagram 117 is a good example; Diagram 118 shows the same principle, but in a more elaborate form.

A Knight fork is often deadly in combination with a pin —as in Diagram 126.

Generally speaking, the most effective Knight forks are checks. Diagram 131 is a fine example: White attacks King and Queen; the King must move; the Queen is lost.

Finally, a Knight fork may often come at the very end of a combination, with an effect which is all the more powerful. See the sequence in Diagram 138, where White's weird-looking preliminary moves take on portentous meaning with the concluding Knight fork.

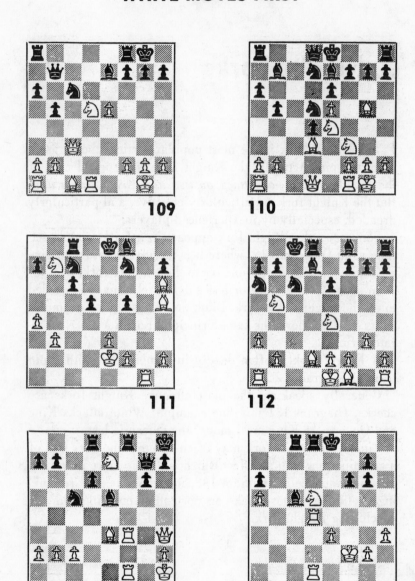

109

110

111

112

113

114

WHITE MOVES FIRST

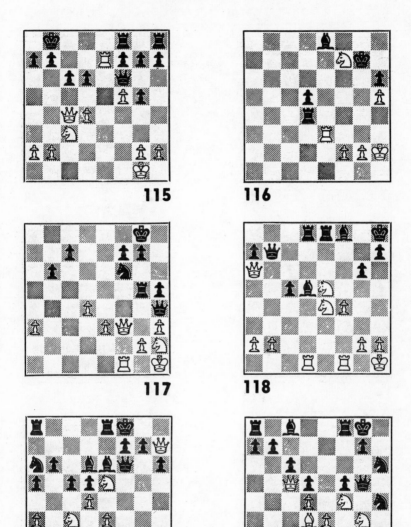

115

116

117

118

119

120

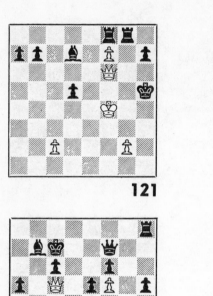

121

122

123

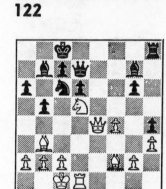

124

125

126

34 · KNIGHT FORKS ·

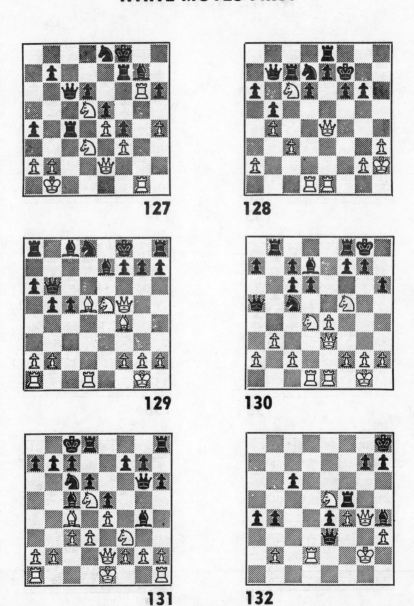

127

128

129

130

131

132

133

134

135

136

137

138

36 · KNIGHT FORKS ·

139

140

141

142

143

144

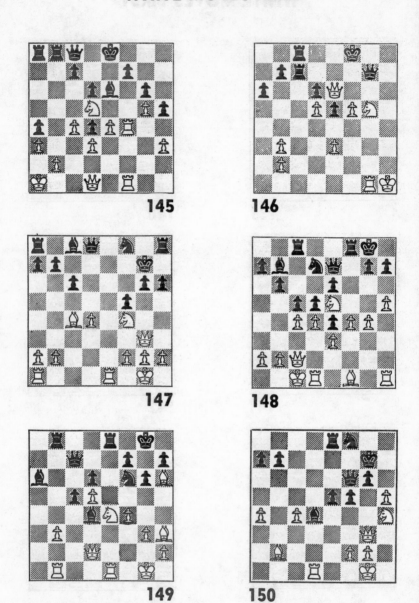

145

146

147

148

149

150

BLACK MOVES FIRST

151

152

153

154

155

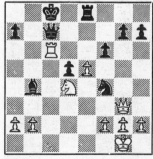

156

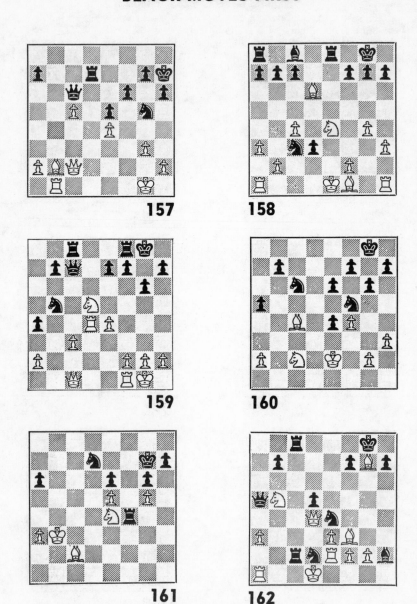

157

158

159

160

161

162

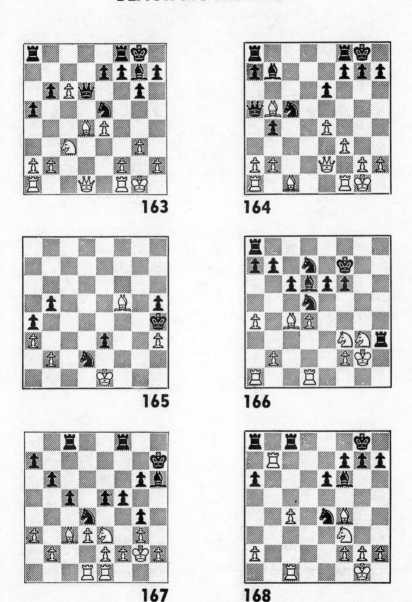

163

164

165

166

167

168

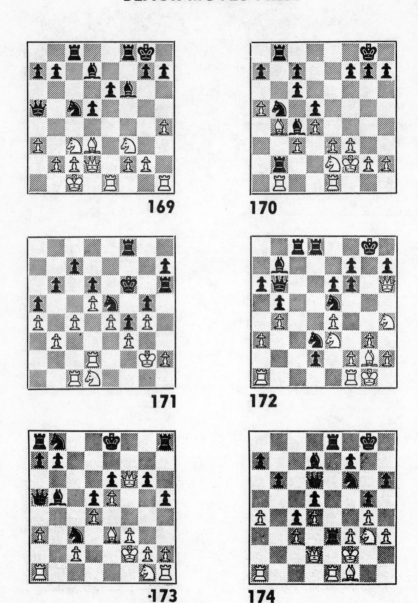

169

170

171

172

·173

174

175

176

177

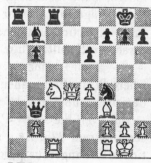

178

179

180

3. Double Attack

This type of attack—*simultaneous attack by a single unit on two hostile units*—is the very essence of chess. This attack is economical and profitable. It appeals to the player who knows how to get the maximum effect from his pieces.

The Queen, with its wide cruising range and ability to attack in several directions by vertical, lateral, and diagonal moves, is the ideal piece for the double attack.

In Diagram 181, for example, the Queen threatens mate in one direction and menaces an unguarded Knight in another direction. Result: White wins a Knight by force.

The same theme is neatly illustrated in Diagram 187, where White first maneuvers the Queen in order to set up the decisive double attack.

But even the lowly Pawn can engineer a double attack—see Diagram 225. As a matter of fact, the Pawn fork is particularly dangerous precisely *because* the Pawn has the least value of any chess unit. Diagram 253 is another splendid illustration of this theme.

The Rook (Diagram 291) and the Bishop (Diagram 277) are also effective in carrying out double attacks.

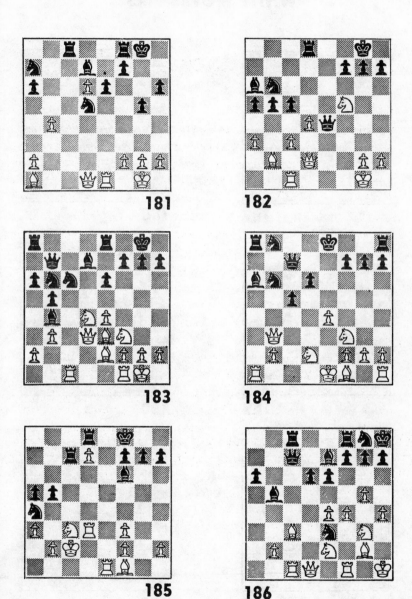

181

182

183

184

185

186

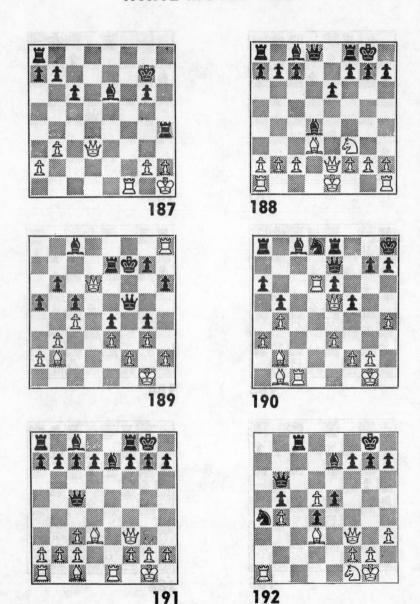

187

188

189

190

191

192

193

194

195

196

197

198

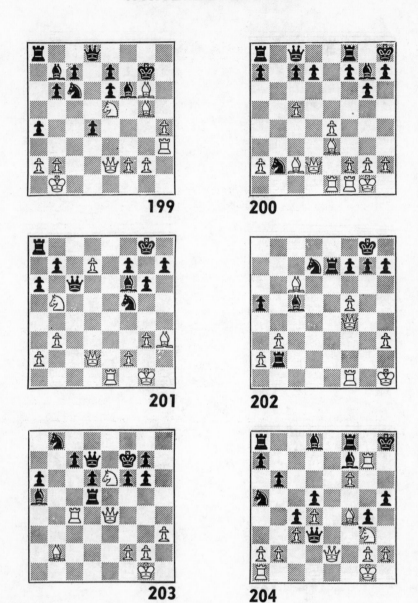

199

200

201

202

203

204

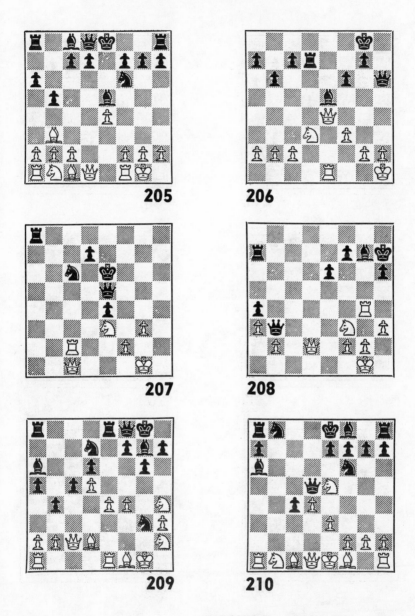

205

206

207

208

209

210

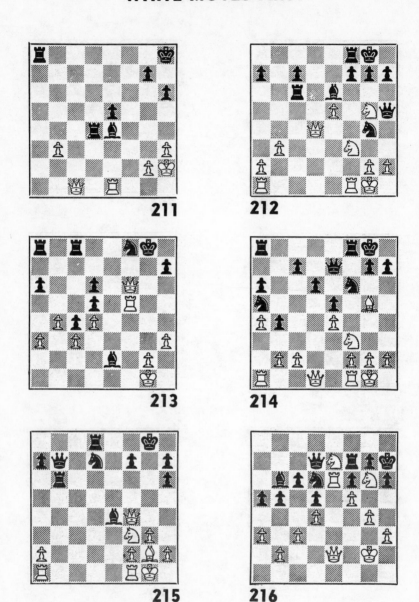

211

212

213

214

215

216

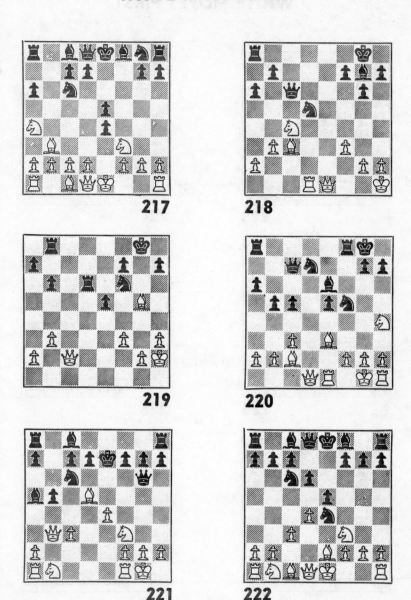

217

218

219

220

221

222

223

224

225

226

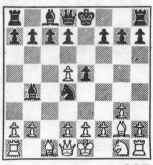

227

228

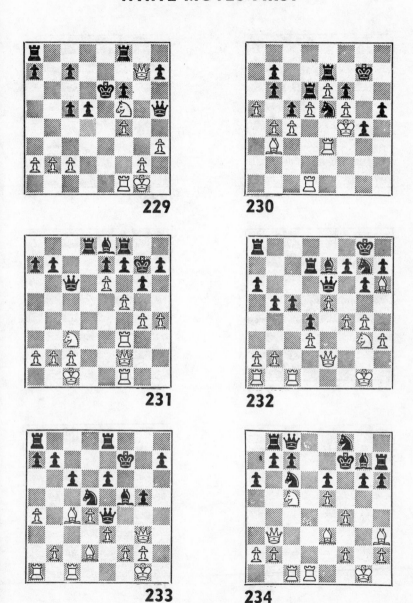

229

230

231

232

233

234

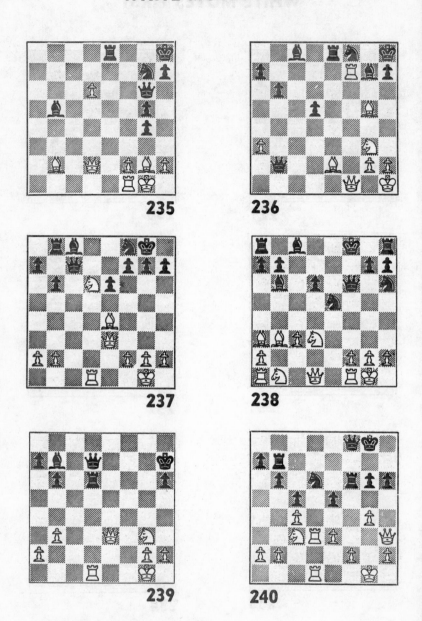

235

236

237

238

239

240

WHITE MOVES FIRST

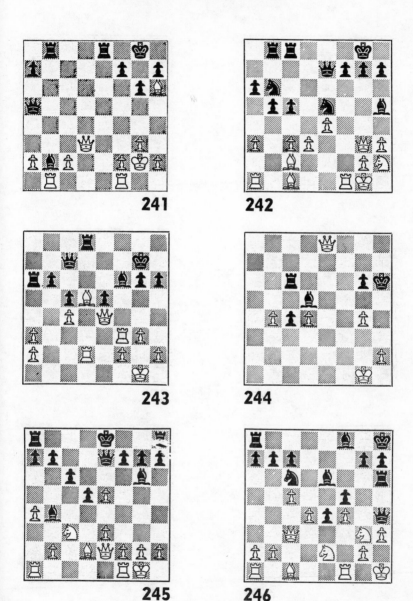

241

242

243

244

245

246

WHITE MOVES FIRST

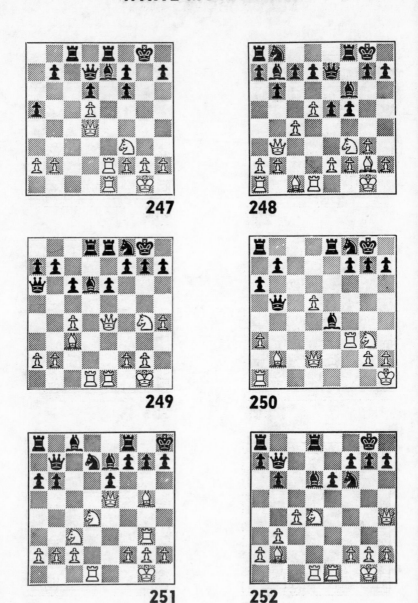

247

248

249

250

251

252

56 · DOUBLE ATTACK ·

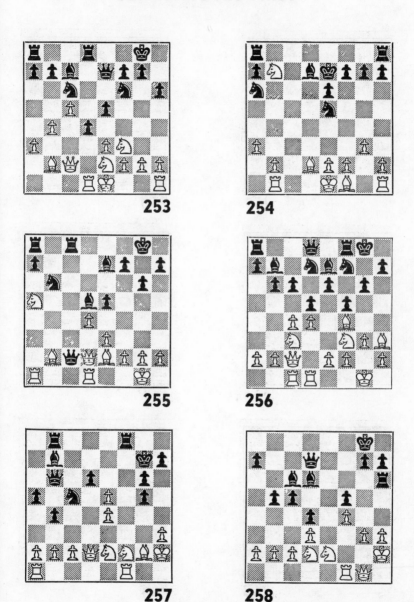

253

254

255

256

257

258

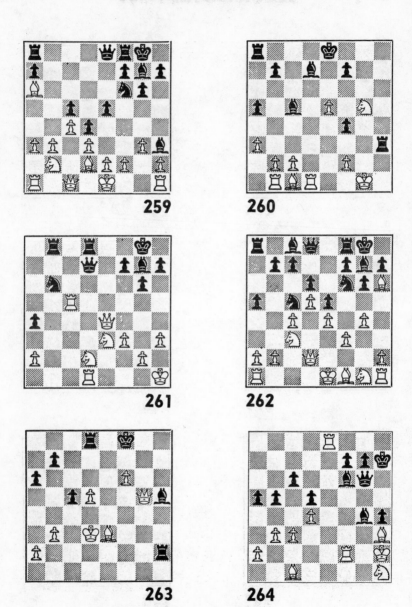

259

260

261

262

263

264

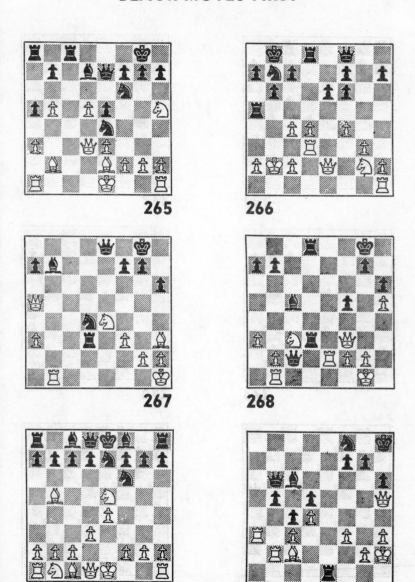

265

266

267

268

269

270

271

272

273

274

275

276

BLACK MOVES FIRST

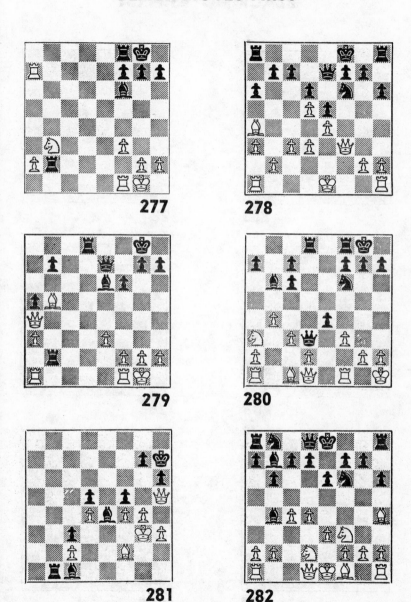

277

278

279

280

281

282

BLACK MOVES FIRST

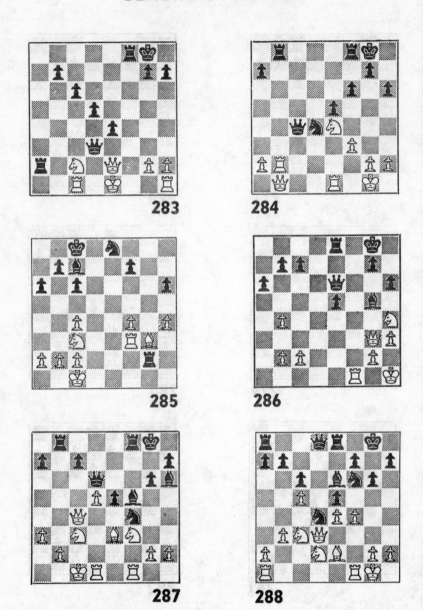

283

284

285

286

287

288

BLACK MOVES FIRST

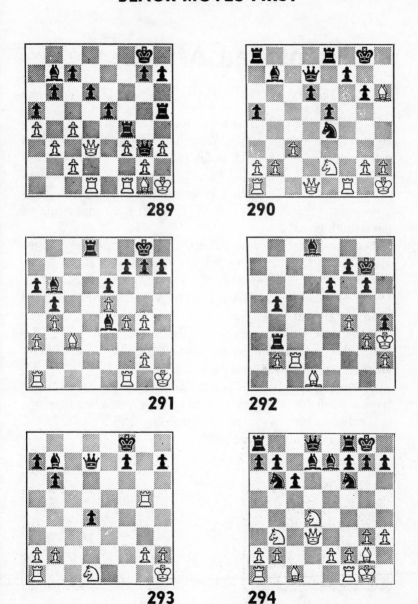

289

290

291

292

293

294

4. Discovered Attack

The discovered attack is an unusually elegant—and powerful—form of double attack. What happens in this case is that *a unit moves off a line in order to "discover"* (actually uncover) *an attack by one of its colleagues.* What usually happens is that the "discovering" piece simultaneously unleashes a secondary threat of its own. Very often it is impossible to parry both threats.

Diagram 295 is a fine example. White's opening Knight move threatens a mate by White's Queen. But at the same time White's Knight menaces Black's Queen, which cannot be saved. The same effect is achieved by White in Diagram 314.

In certain rare instances, as in Diagram 321, we get enchanting effects when multiple threats are opened up. The inexorable beauty of these situations is that the defender has all sorts of resources—but each one fails!

Discovered attacks are particularly nasty when they arise from a plausible series of preliminary moves. When they are concealed in this way, as in Diagrams 325 and 327, the defender is virtually paralyzed.

WHITE MOVES FIRST

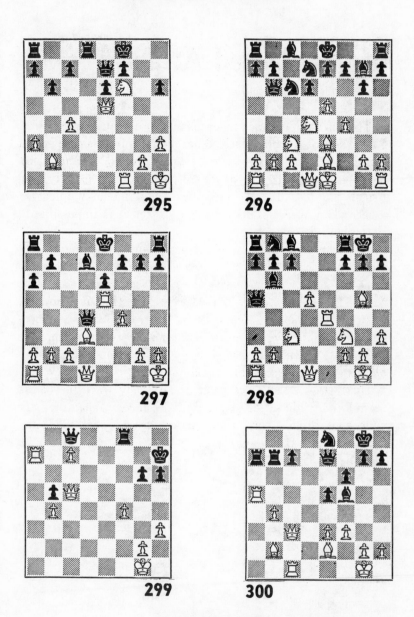

295

296

297

298

299

300

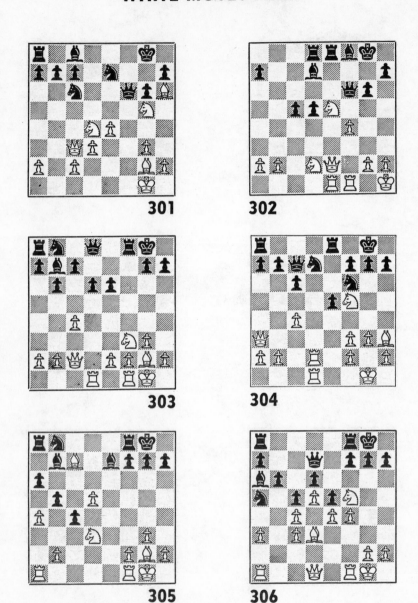

301

302

303

304

305

306

307

308

309

310

311

312

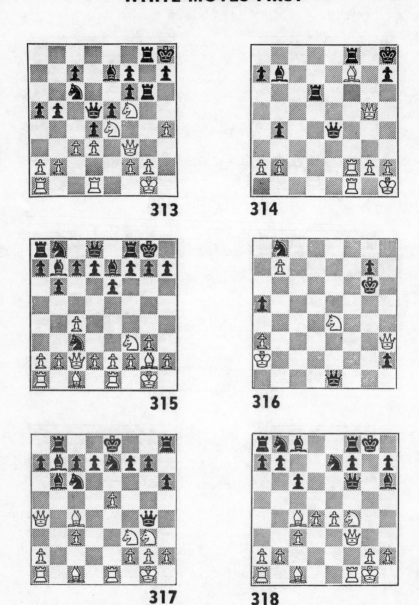

313

314

315

316

317

318

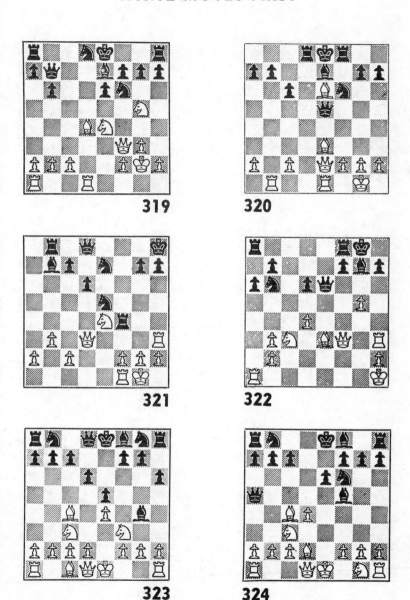

319

320

321

322

323

324

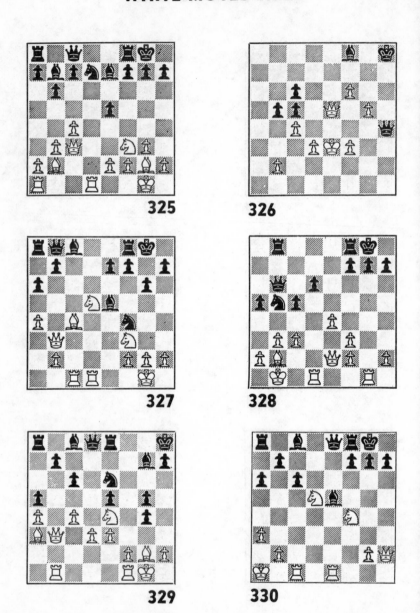

325

326

327

328

329

330

BLACK MOVES FIRST

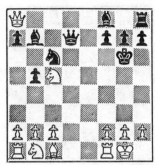

331

332

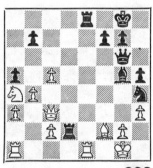

333

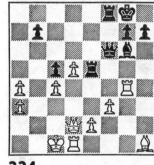

334

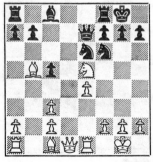

335

336

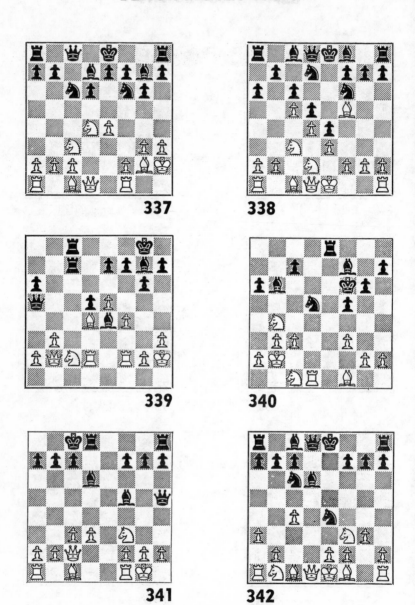

337

338

339

340

341

342

BLACK MOVES FIRST

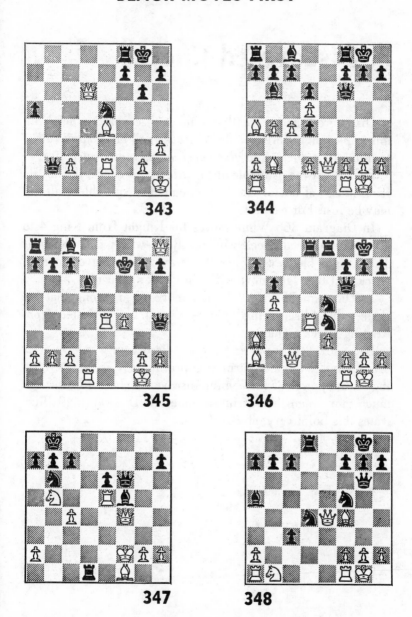

343

344

345

346

347

348

5. Discovered Check

Discovered check is really a kind of discovered attack, with this important difference: *the "discovering" piece moves away to allow its colleague to give check along the vacated line.*

Because of the principle of the priority of check, the hostile King must get out of check. Consequently valuable material may be lost. For example:

In Diagram 366 White moves his Knight from King 4 to give a discovered check with his Rook which is at King 1. The Knight has several possible ways of giving discovered check, but the right move will win Black's Queen.

In Diagram 357 White's first move is so strong that his Rook—the "discovering" piece—cannot be prevented from winning Black's Queen.

Because of this power of the "discovering" piece, it is often possible to make surprising preliminary sacrifices, relying on the power of the coming discovered check to win back much more than the sacrificed material. Diagram 349 illustrates this point very effectively.

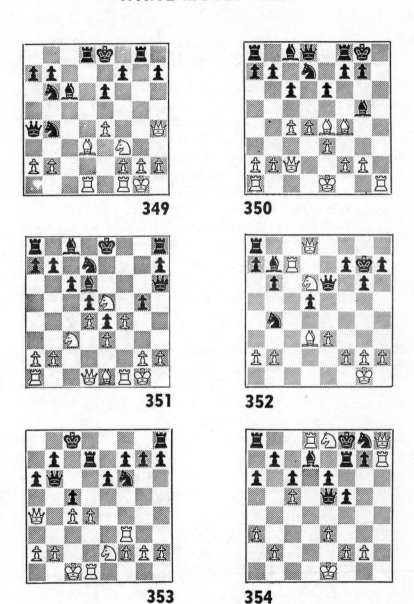

349

350

351

352

353

354

WHITE MOVES FIRST

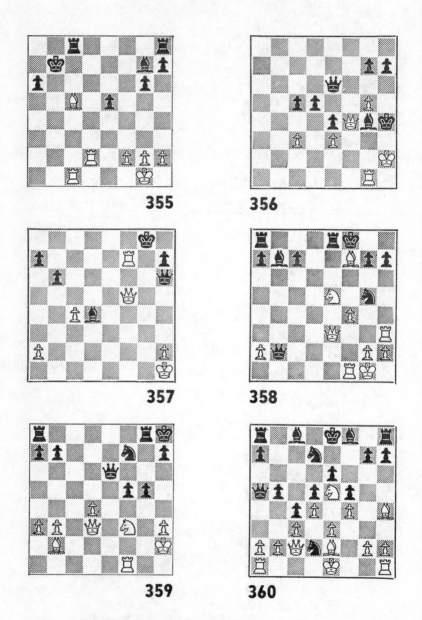

355

356

357

358

359

360

76 · DISCOVERED CHECK ·

361

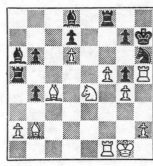

362

363

364

365

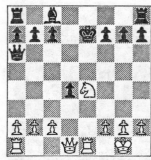

366

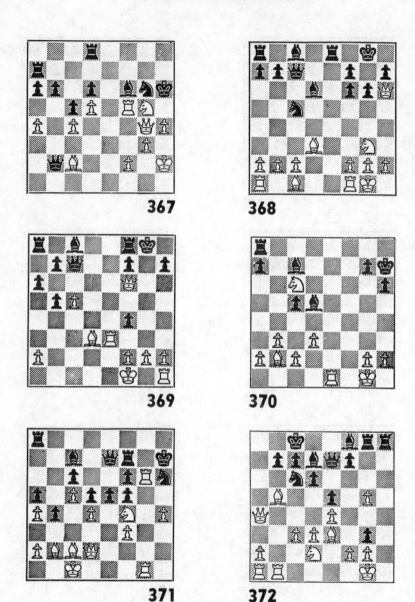

367

368

369

370

371

372

WHITE MOVES FIRST

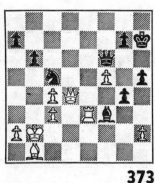

373

374

375

376

377

378

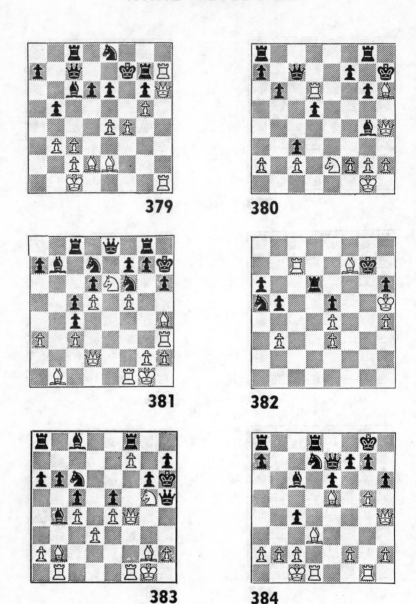

379

380

381

382

383

384

BLACK MOVES FIRST

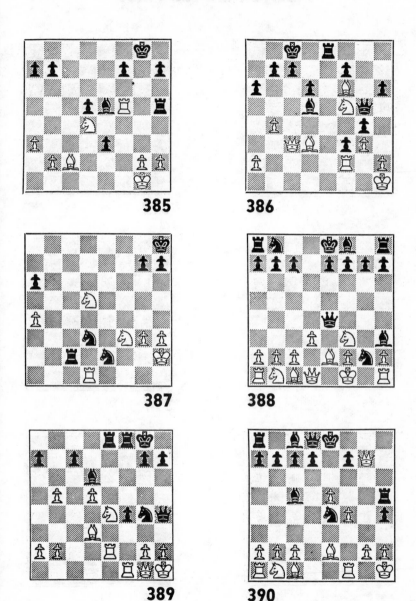

385

386

387

388

389

390

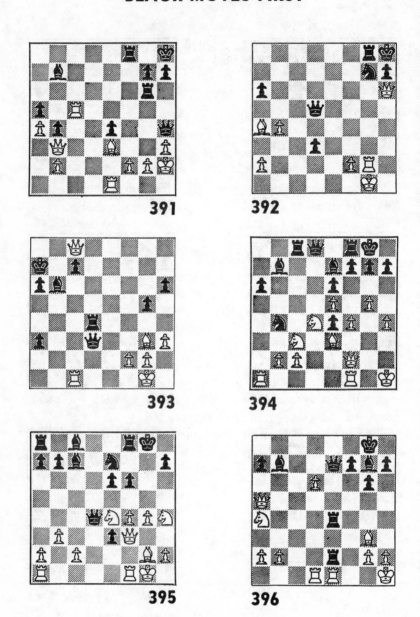

391

392

393

394

395

396

6. Double Check

Of all the different kinds of discovered check, the double check is the most dangerous and the most menacing. *For here the "discovering" piece not only uncovers a check; by moving, it gives a direct check.*

This is the most drastic situation that ever confronts a King; for in the case of double check, capture or interposition is impossible. The only way to answer a double check is by moving the King.

Because of its formidable power, the double check has made possible some of the most glamorous combinations in the whole range of chess literature. Diagram 399 is a characteristic example. First comes a completely unexpected Queen sacrifice, followed by a double check with Rook and Bishop, and checkmate next move.

Queen sacrifices are quite common in this section, for the mighty double check easily makes up for the sacrificed material. There are other aritstic possibilities as well, the most beautiful of all appearing in Diagram 407.

Very often the double check brusquely triumphs over hostile attacks, as in the startling finish in Diagram 417. Never underestimate the power of a double check!

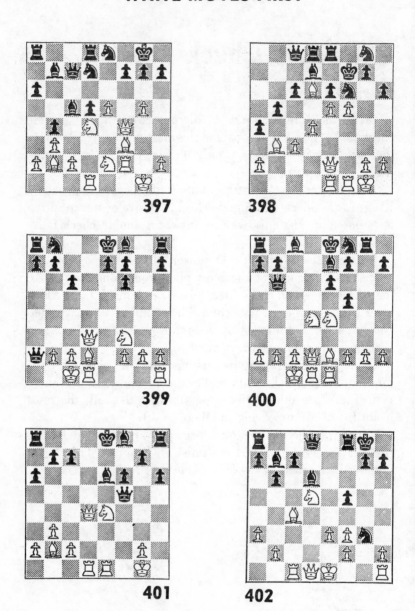

397   398

399   400

401   402

WHITE MOVES FIRST

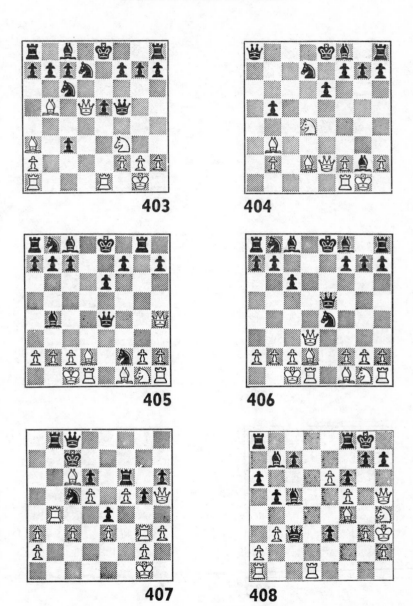

403

404

405

406

407

408

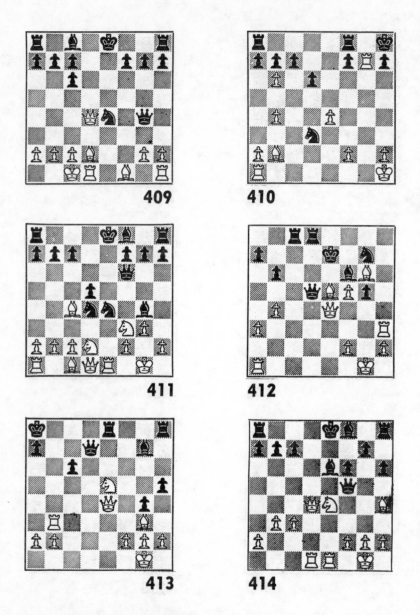

409 410

411 412

413 414

BLACK MOVES FIRST

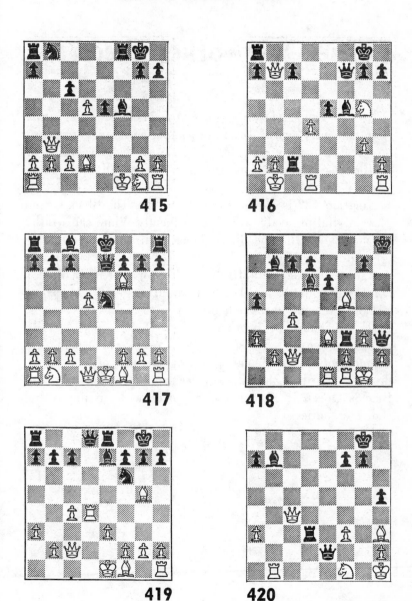

415

416

417

418

419

420

7. The Overworked Piece

No man can serve two masters. And in chess, *no piece can simultaneously guard two pieces without becoming a target of attack*. The principle is clear and simple: a piece which is performing more than one function is especially vulnerable to hostile attack.

Diagram 422 is a good example of this. The Black Queen plays a vital protective role. Consequently White can win by constantly harrying the Black Queen until it is forced to give up its protective function.

Again, in Diagram 430, Black's Bishop at King Knight 2 is given the unwelcome choice of capturing White's Queen or Bishop, allowing checkmate in either case. In other words, Black's Bishop is overworked.

In Diagram 437 Black's Knight is overworked, being unable to capture White's checking Rook because of its primary duty of guarding the Black Queen. And in Diagram 440 Black's Queen is an overworked piece with an impossible choice of duties!

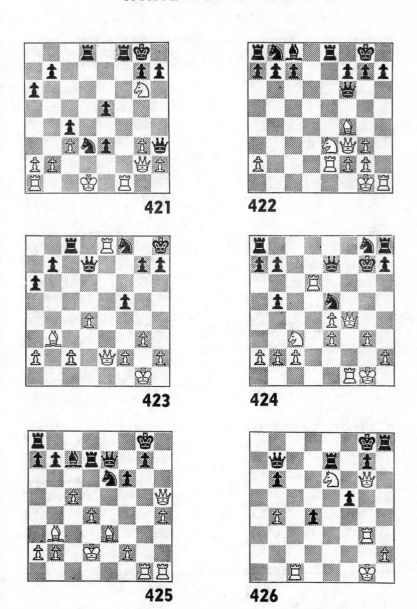

421

422

423

424

425

426

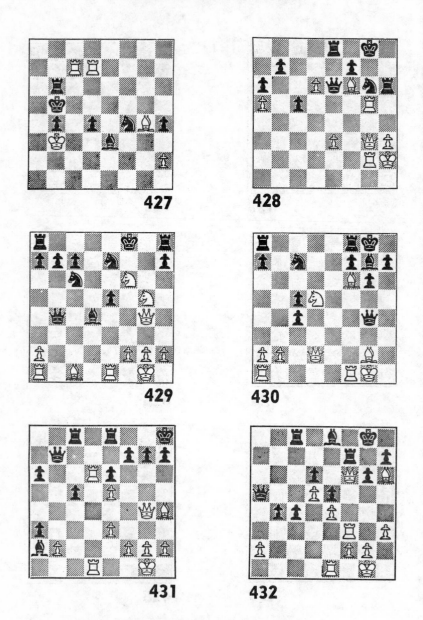

427

428

429

430

431

432

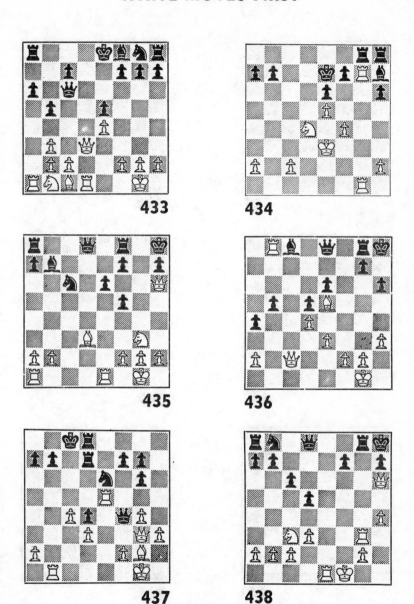

433

434

435

436

437

438

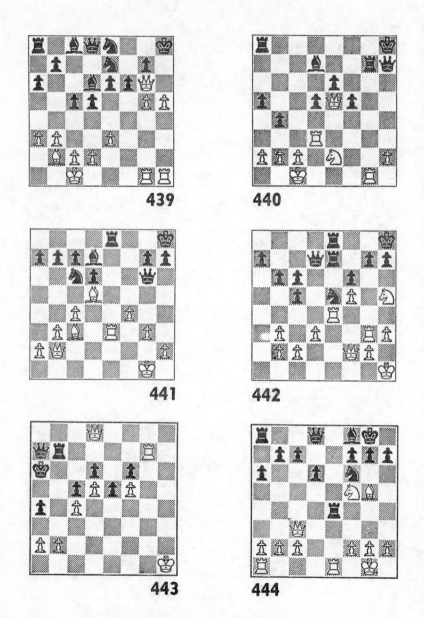

439

440

441

442

443

444

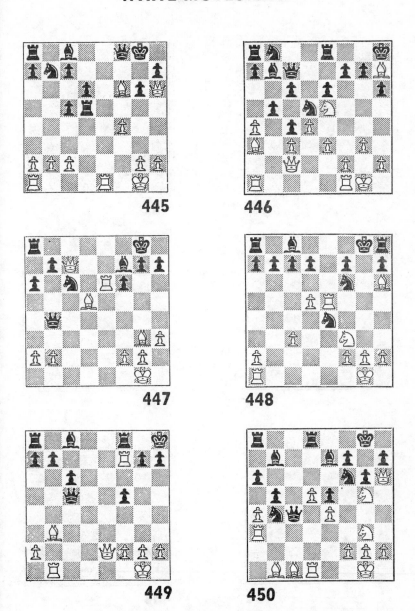

445

446

447

448

449

450

WHITE MOVES FIRST

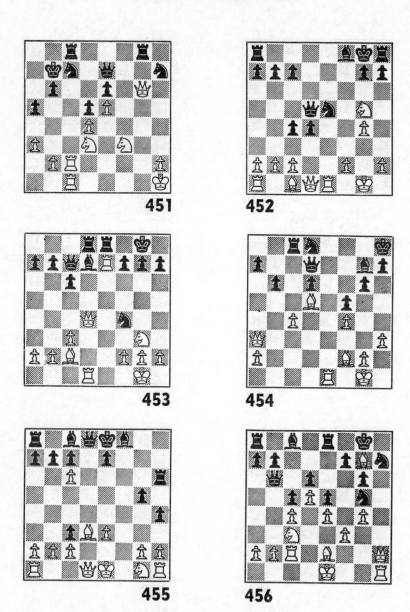

451

452

453

454

455

456

94 · The OVERWORKED PIECE ·

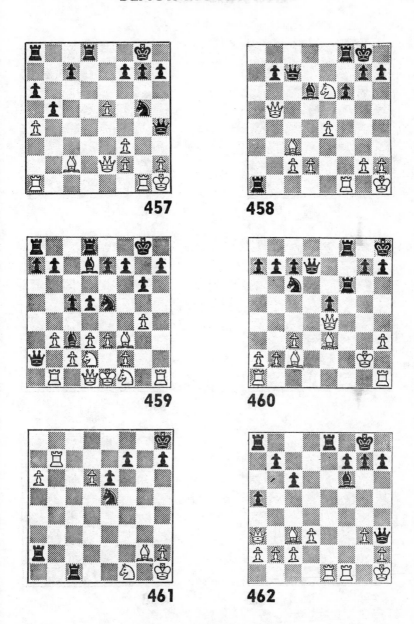

457

458

459

460

461

462

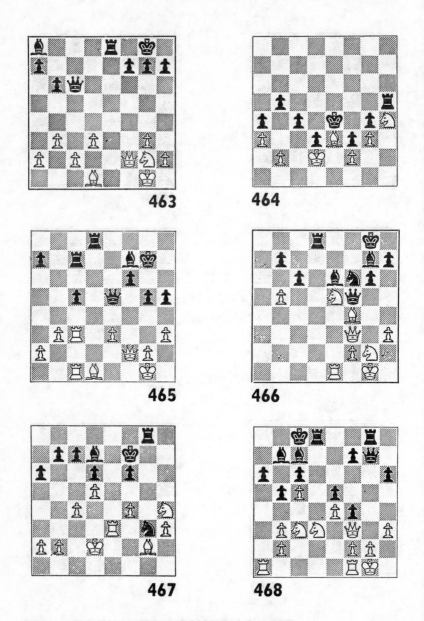

463

464

465

466

467

468

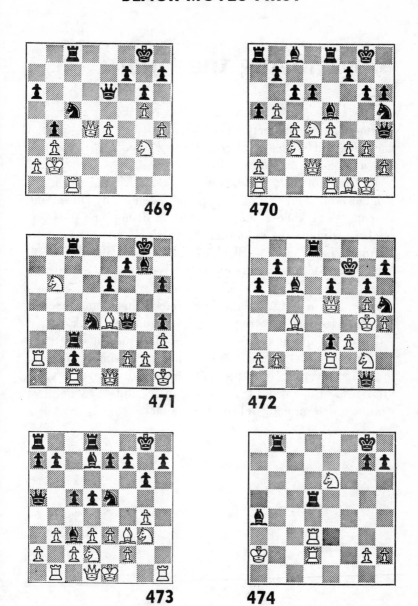

469

470

471

472

473

474

8. Removing the Guard

The principle underlying this theme is the very essence of chess logic. *If Piece A guards Piece B, attack Piece A and you win one or the other.*

In Diagram 477, for example, Black's Knight at King 5 is attacked by Queen and Bishop and defended by Queen and Bishop. White knocks out the protective Bishop and thus succeeds in winning the vulnerable Knight.

And in Diagram 484, Black's Rook protects Black's Queen. But not for long, for White immediately removes the guardian Rook.

Note also in Diagram 486 how Black's guardian Queen is removed, forcing the win of Black's unguarded Rook.

Removing the guard is one of the most useful of all the tactical themes. In chess, there is no surer winning method than concentrating on hostile units that are tied down to some vital task. Deprived of mobility, these units are helpless against a determined, well directed attack.

WHITE MOVES FIRST

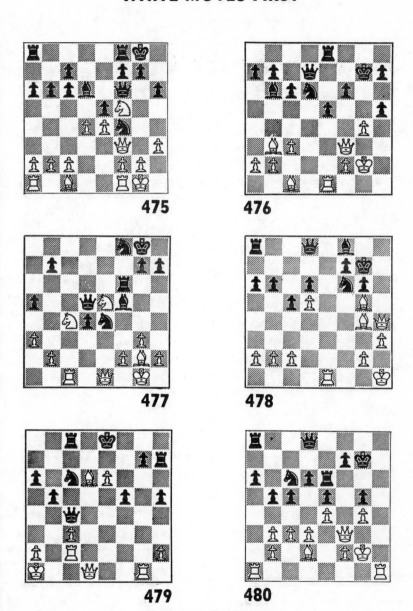

475

476

477

478

479

480

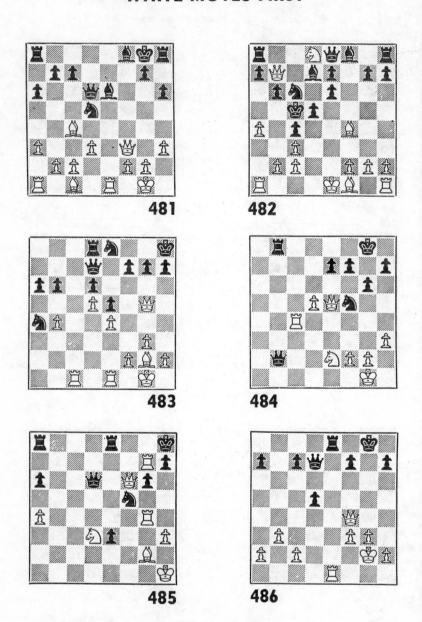

481

482

483

484

485

486

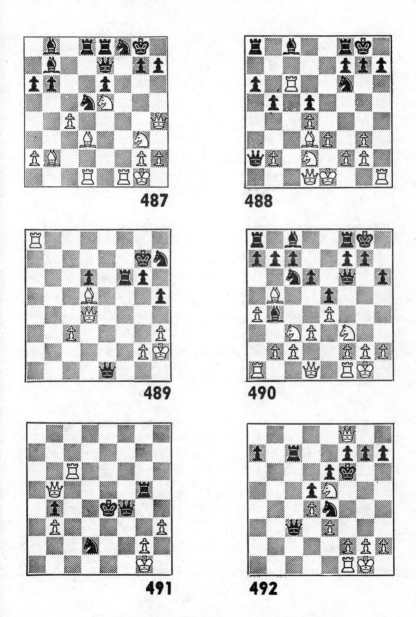

487

488

489

490

491

492

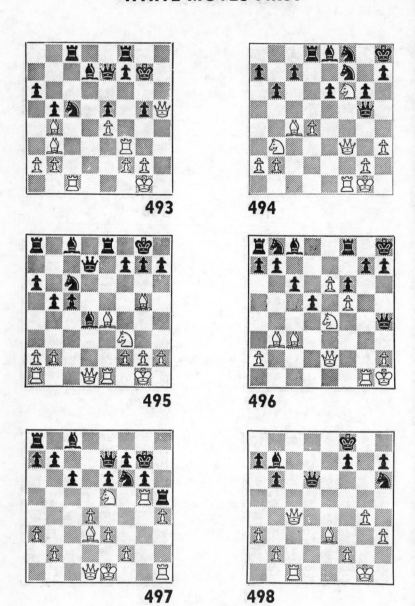

493

494

495

496

497

498

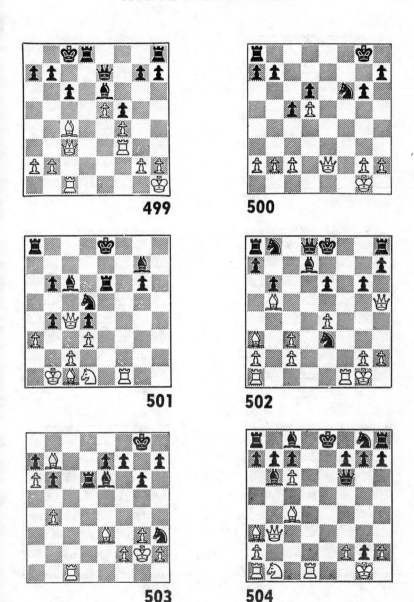

499

500

501

502

503

504

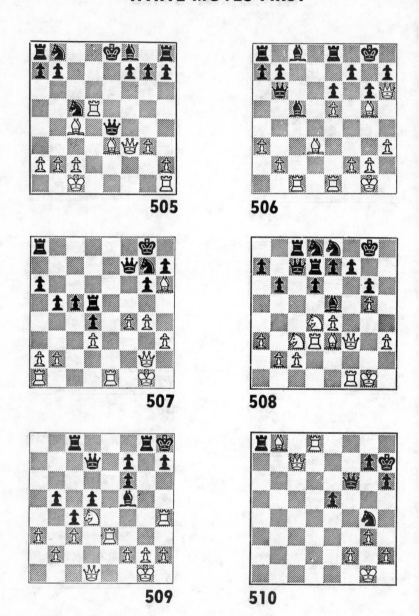

505

506

507

508

509

510

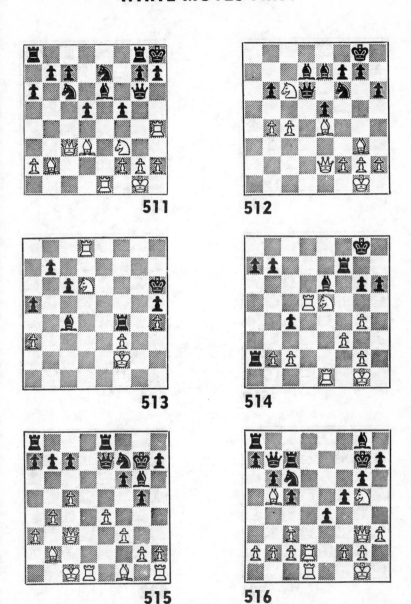

511

512

513

514

515

516

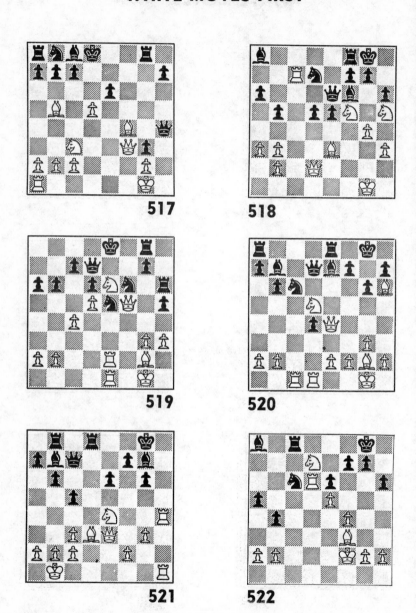

517

518

519

520

521

522

BLACK MOVES FIRST

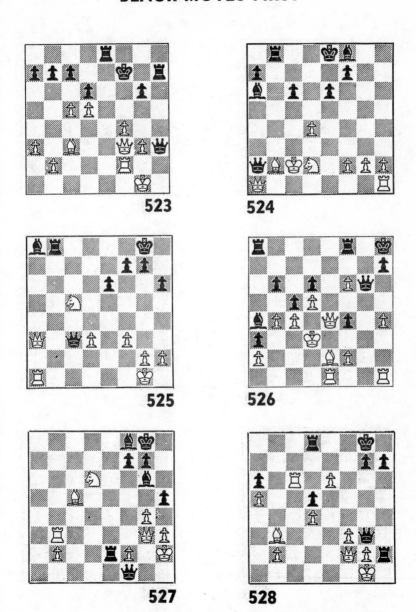

523

524

525

526

527

528

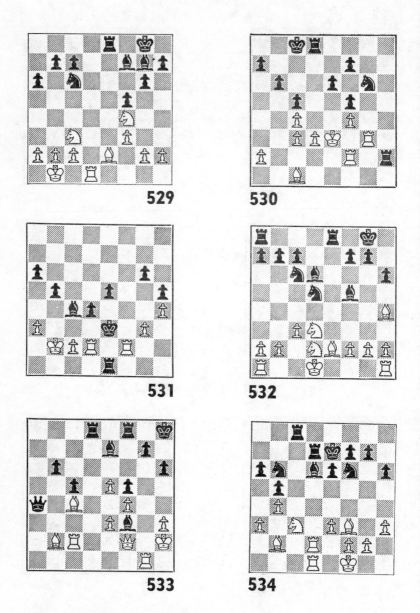

529

530

531

532

533

534

BLACK MOVES FIRST

535

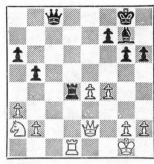

536

537

538

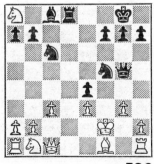

539

540

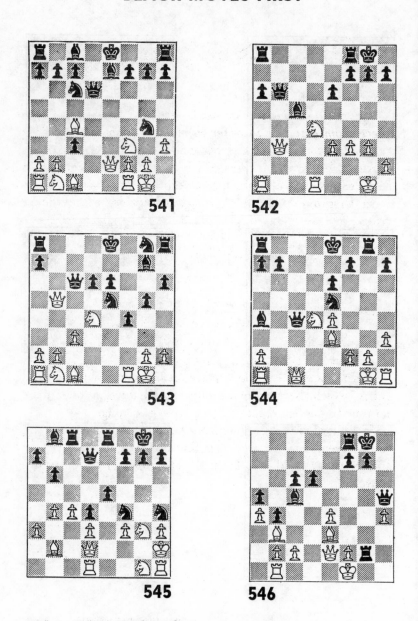

541

542

543

544

545

546

9. Clearance

Clearance is the term we use to describe *the removal of a piece from a square in order to make that square available to another unit.* Often this occupation by the new piece involves a decisive attack, hence we clear the square even if it involves a spectacular sacrifice of material.

In Diagram 547, for example, White clears the square King 5 by sacrificing his Knight. But the Knight move looks senseless, and it is followed by a Queen sacrifice that looks more spectacular and even more senseless. However, there follows a terrific double check and Black cannot escape checkmate! Then all the moves of the combination appear in their proper perspective, and we see that the initial clearance move was really a stroke of genius. Observe, by the way, that this clearance move involved an attack on Black's Queen and thus left him no time to rearrange his forces for adequate defense.

In Diagram 549 White's clearance maneuver depends on a check, which, because of its imperious nature, allows Black no time to prevent White's Pawn from queening.

In general, you will note that a good clearance move is apt to be peremptory. The point is that the defender is given no time to parry the threat that is the real point of the clearance move.

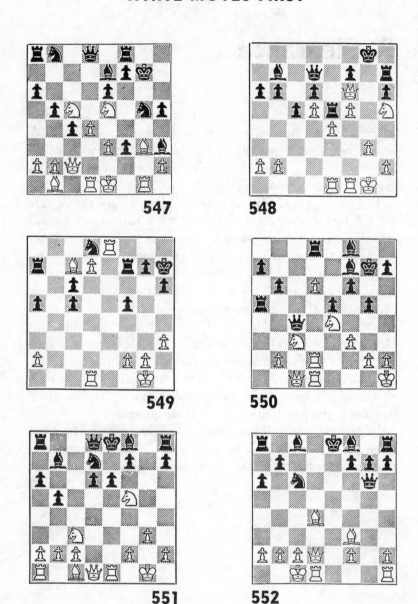

547

548

549

550

551

552

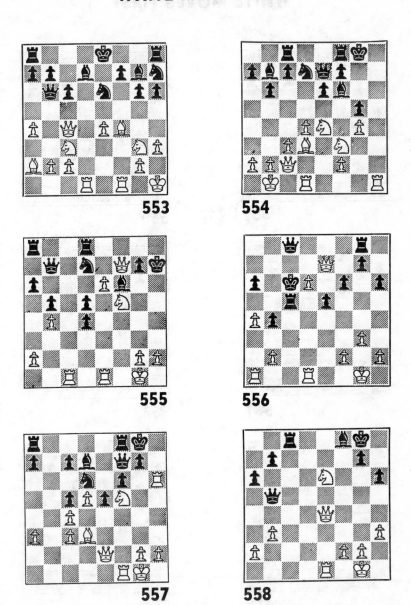

553

554

555

556

557

558

559

560

561

562

563

564

WHITE MOVES FIRST

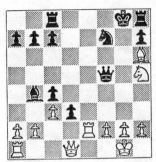

565

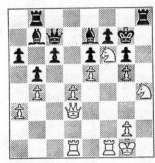

566

567

568

569

570

WHITE MOVES FIRST

571

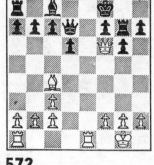

572

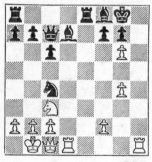

573

574

575

576

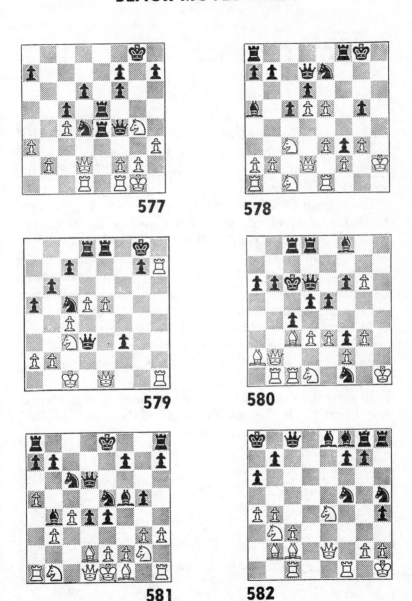

577

578

579

580

581

582

10. Interference

Interference, as the term indicates, occurs where *the defender is forced to block himself*. He has a choice of moving two pieces to a critical square. Whichever piece he moves, he blocks the operations of the other piece and is thus left helpless against his opponent's threats.

In Diagram 583, for example, White's first move presents Black with a cruel dilemma. If he captures the obnoxious Rook with his King Pawn, he allows himself to be mated. And if he captures with his Queen, the result is the same.

Even more artistic is the setting of Diagram 604, where the defender is presented with a number of choices, each leading to a pretty checkmate.

In Diagram 606 White's use of the interference theme is especially subtle, the idea being to create a block on White's King 5 square so that Black cannot save himself by playing ... Q—B4ch.

In general, the interference theme produces a large proportion of artistic conclusions. This is due to the finesse involved in forcing the defender's pieces to destroy each other's working ability.

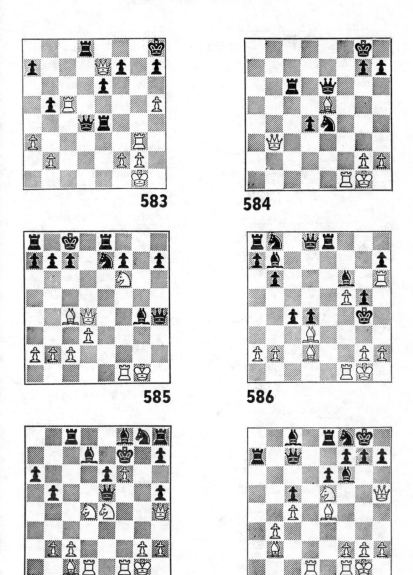

583

584

585

586

587

588

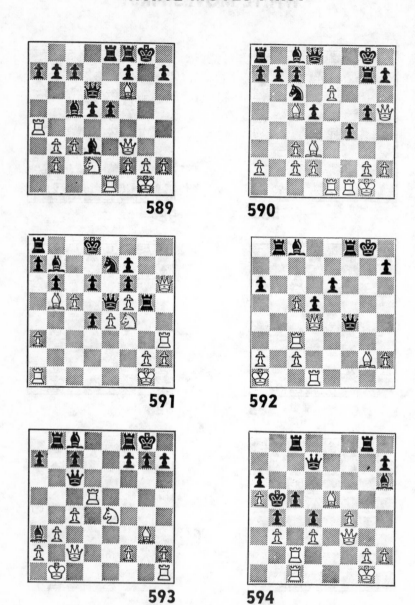

589

590

591

592

593

594

WHITE MOVES FIRST

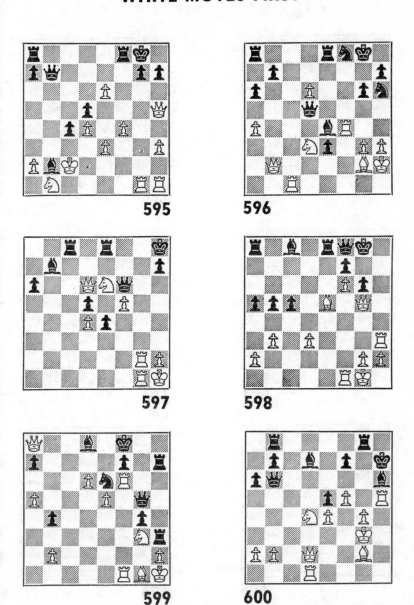

595

596

597

598

599

600

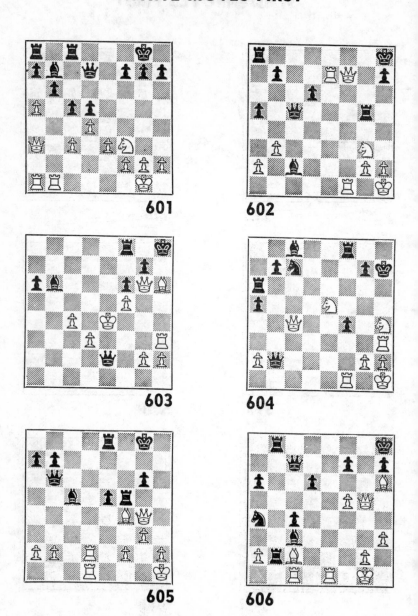

601

602

603

604

605

606

BLACK MOVES FIRST

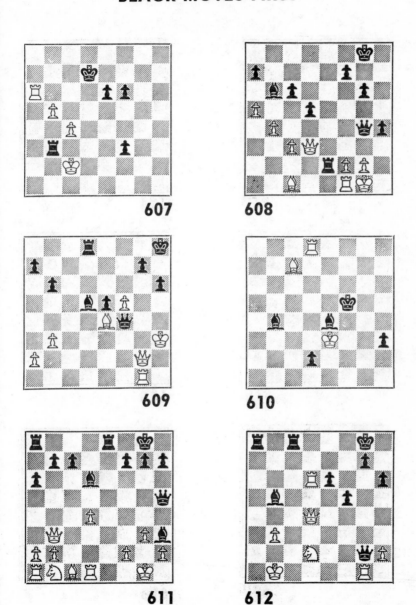

607

608

609

610

611

612

BLACK MOVES FIRST

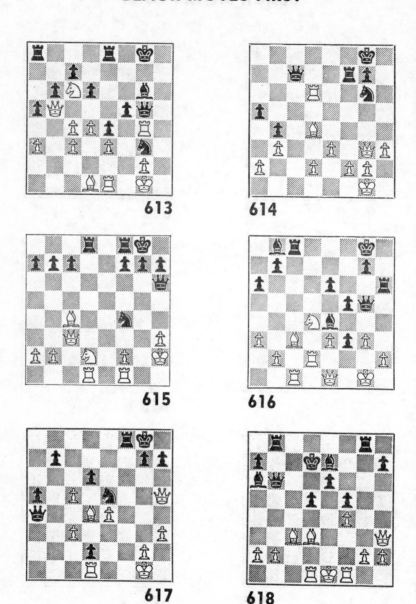

613

614

615

616

617

618

BLACK MOVES FIRST

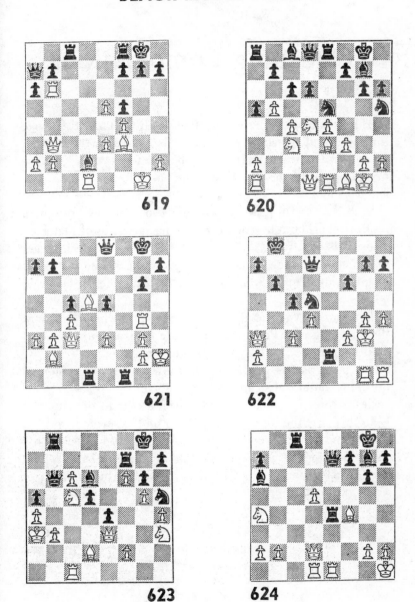

619

620

621

622

623

624

II. Queening Combinations

This is one of the most important of all the tactical themes, for successful queening of a Pawn is equivalent to being a Queen ahead. And even if your opponent loses "only" a piece in getting rid of the new Queen, he has suffered a disastrous material loss.

Since successful Pawn promotion is so valuable a resource, it offers considerable scope for striking sacrifices of material. Thus, it is well worth while to sacrifice one's Queen in order to promote to a new Queen which gives checkmate in the act of queening. This is what happens, for example, in Diagram 645.

Diagram 631 is one of the many examples which show how the queening of a Pawn may lead to a decisive gain of material. Diagram 625 illustrates the same motif.

Diagram 648 is interesting as showing how the potential queening possibility can inspire a player to create a whole series of pretty tactical strokes. Given a *clue* to the situation —in this case the location of a Pawn on the seventh rank—a player can think up one resourceful move after another. But the initial impetus is most important of all, and that is why it is of great value to be well aware of the enormous power of Pawn promotion.

WHITE MOVES FIRST

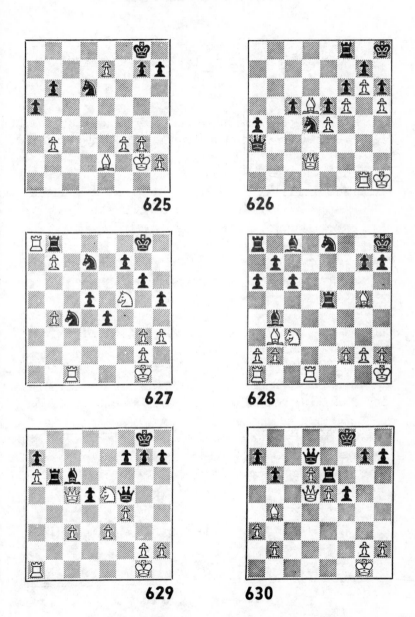

625

626

627

628

629

630

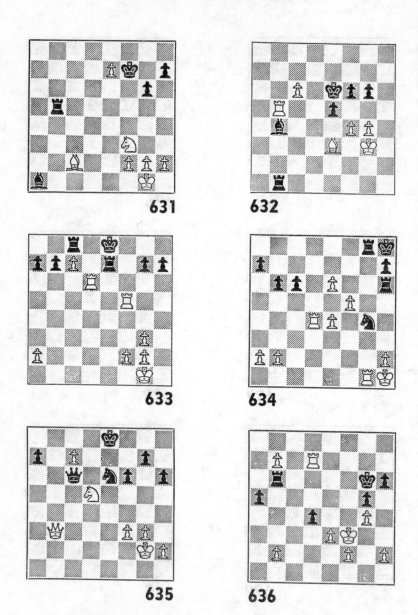

631

632

633

634

635

636

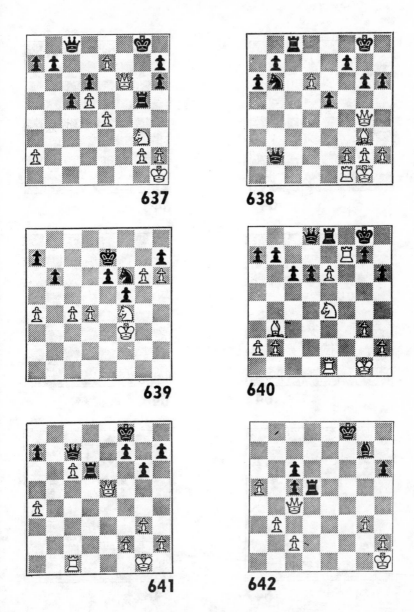

637

638

639

640

641

642

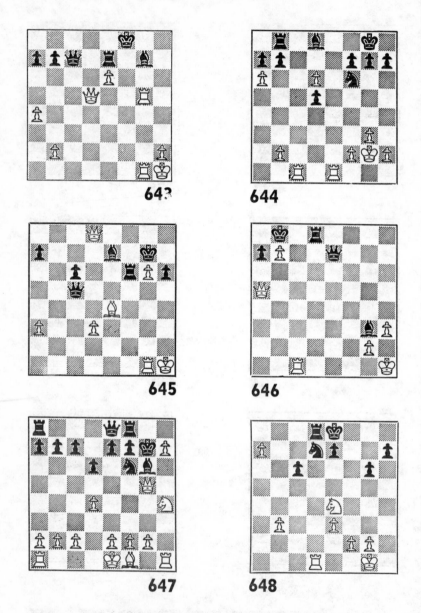

643

644

645

646

647

648

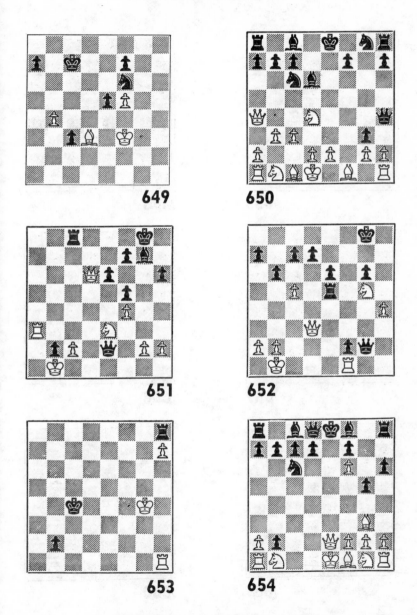

649

650

651

652

653

654

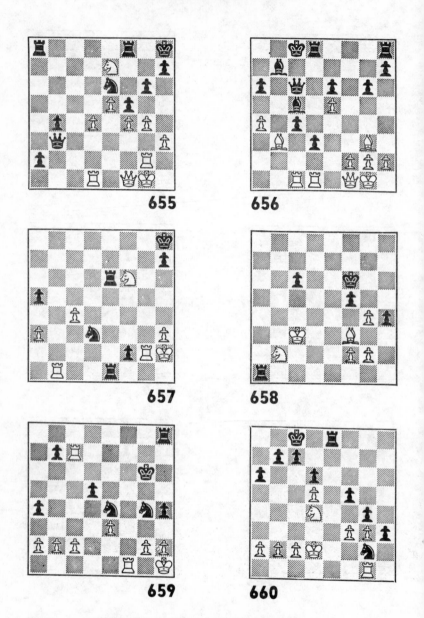

655

656

657

658

659

660

BLACK MOVES FIRST

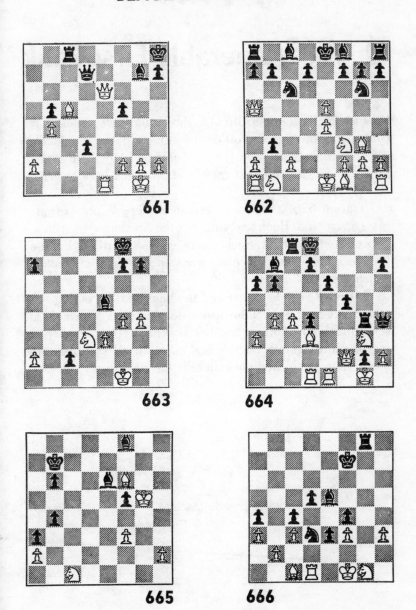

661

662

663

664

665

666

12. The Vulnerable First Rank

Some of the most brilliant combinations ever made have come about through exploiting the vulnerable first rank. This happens when the castled King is hemmed in by the Pawns in front of him, and his first rank is unprotected by a Queen or Rook.

Diagram 676 is a perfect example. Here White can offer his Queen and Rook, relying on the weakness of Black's unprotected first rank. Such sacrifices look startling, but they become quite obvious once you are familiar with the weakness which they exploit.

This is effectively illustrated in Diagram 679, perhaps the most famous of all combinations devoted to this theme. One sensational move follows another as White relies on his crushing pressure against White's first rank. In all such cases the hostile King's blocked position tells the story.

WHITE MOVES FIRST

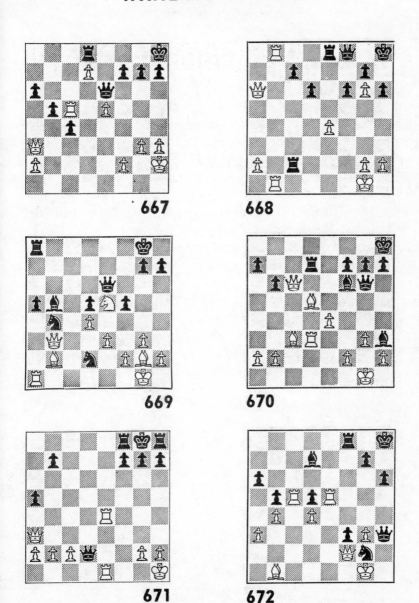

667

668

669

670

671

672

WHITE MOVES FIRST

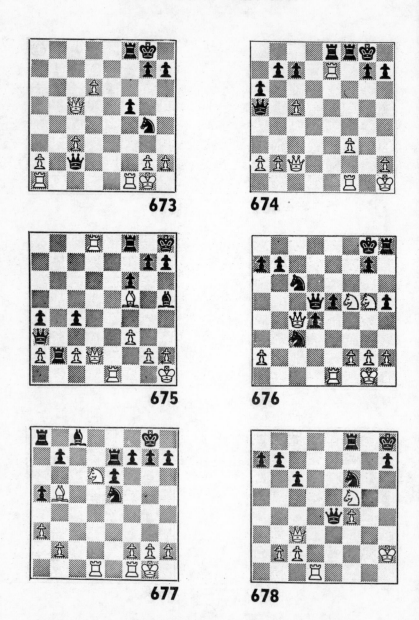

673

674

675

676

677

678

136 · The VULNERABLE FIRST RANK ·

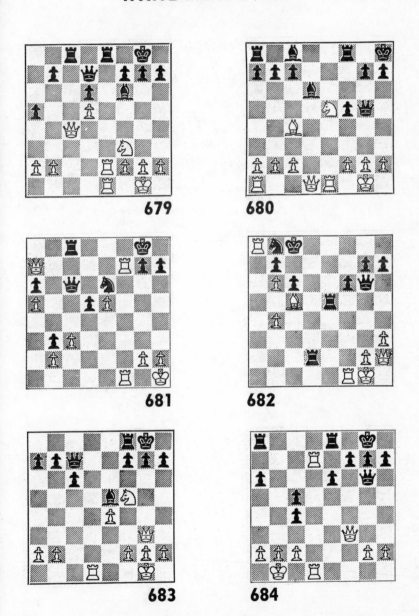

679

680

681

682

683

684

BLACK MOVES FIRST

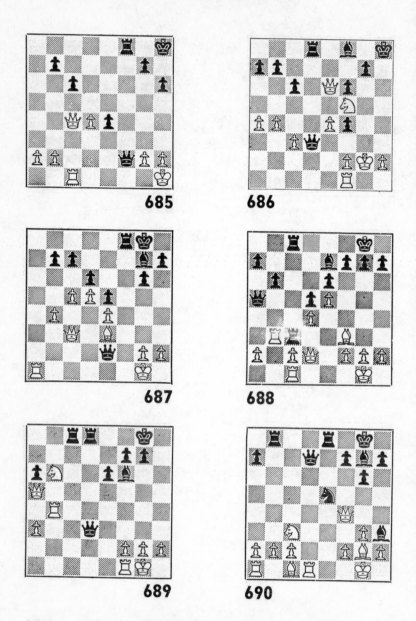

685

686

687

688

689

690

BLACK MOVES FIRST

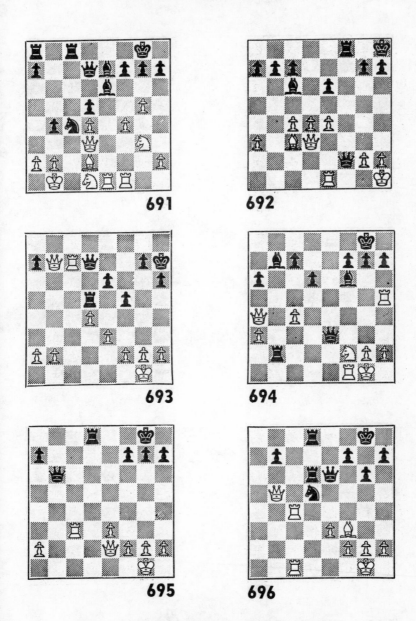

691

692

693

694

695

696

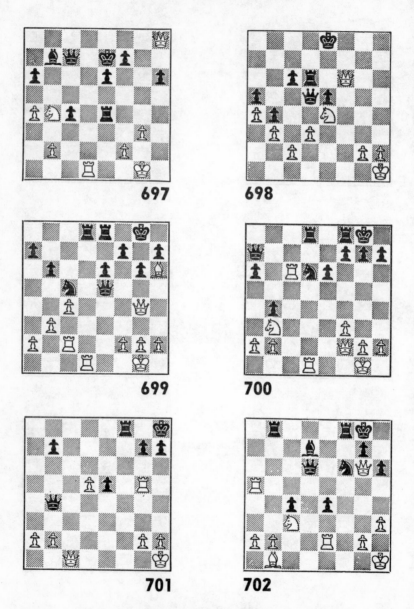

697

698

699

700

701

702

13. Queen Sacrifices

No matter how experienced and sophisticated a chessplayer may be, he is always thrilled by a Queen sacrifice. This is understandable, for the Queen is far and away the strongest of all the chess forces.

Precisely because the Queen is so powerful, the sacrifice of this piece must necessarily bring in substantial returns. Mate is usually the sequel, as for example in Diagram 703, where White offers the Queen in a manner which is surprising but hardly generous. He threatens mate, and when the Queen is captured, he mates just the same. Still, such a sacrifice deserves our praise, for it takes real imagination to see the possibilities in such a position.

What is even more admirable is a Queen sacrifice which leads to a fairly long-winded mate. In Diagram 708, for example, White's Queen sacrifice looks like a typographical error. Who would dream that after the Queen sacrifice White has a forced mate in five moves, making use of Rooks and minor pieces—and even a "lowly" Pawn that draws the Black King into a mating net.

Perhaps even more striking are those Queen sacrifices which are followed up by a series of inspired moves—all with the purpose of winning a . . . mere Pawn! Diagram 734 shows such a combination, which was rightly awarded a First Brilliancy Prize.

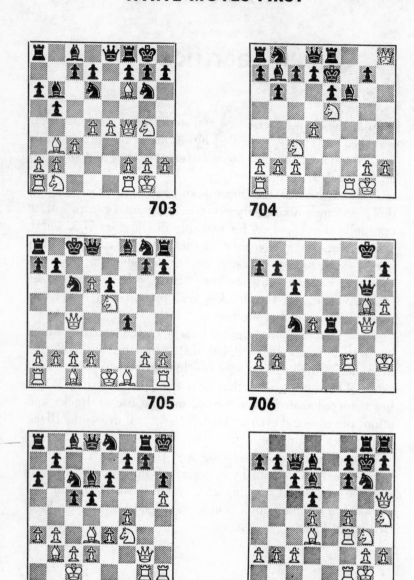

703

704

705

706

707

708

WHITE MOVES FIRST

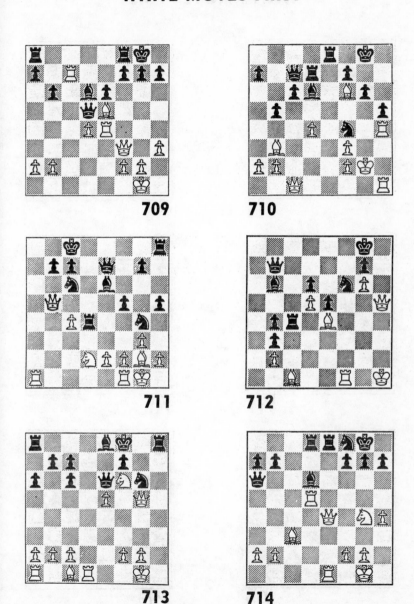

709

710

711

712

713

714

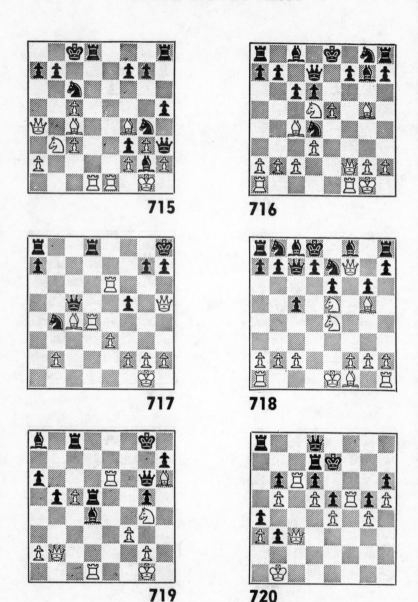

715

716

717

718

719

720

WHITE MOVES FIRST

721

722

723

724

725

726

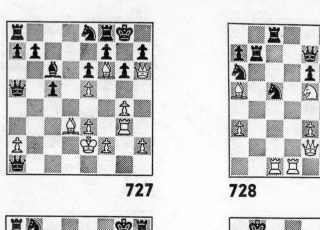

727

728

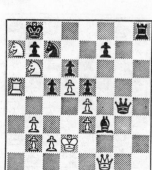

729

730

731

732

733

734

735

736

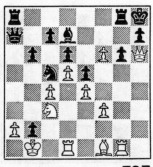

737

738

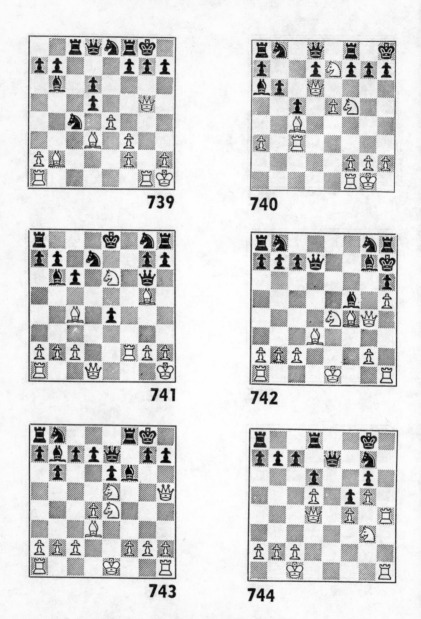

739

740

741

742

743

744

BLACK MOVES FIRST

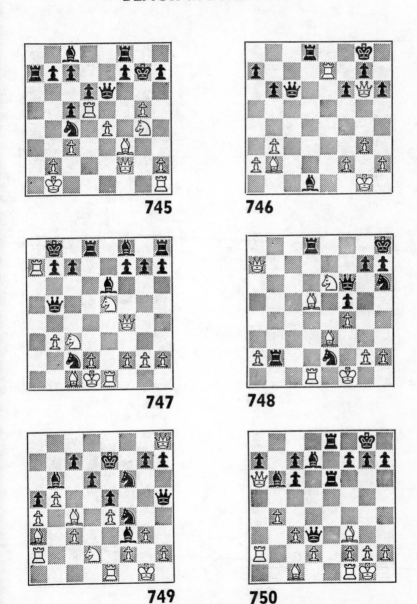

745

746

747

748

749

750

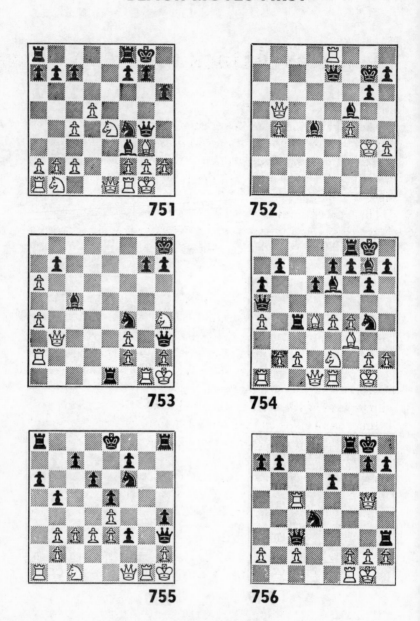

751

752

753

754

755

756

14. X-Ray Attack

The X-ray attack, or skewer attack, is the opposite of the pin. In the X-ray attack, *a piece attacks a hostile piece which is situated on a line with another piece of lesser value*. When the attacked piece moves off the line, it exposes the second piece to capture.

This concept may sound complicated, but an example will show its simplicity—and deadly effectiveness. In Diagram 757 White's Rook maneuvers the Black forces into an X-ray position. Thereupon White's Rook X-rays the Black King, and thus wins the Black Rook.

In Diagram 759 White sets up an X-ray position by sacrificing the Exchange as a preliminary to X-raying the Black King and thereby winning the Black Queen.

Diagram 769 illustrates what is perhaps the most beautiful of all X-ray combinations. Here White sacrifices both Rooks in order to carry out a series of X-ray threats which wind up with the win of Black's Queen. And this comes just in the nick of time, as Black is on the point of administering checkmate!

As explained in the first paragraph, the piece initially menaced by the X-ray is the more important piece. Usually, therefore, the X-ray move is a check (an attack on the King). However, the X-ray may menace other pieces as well. In Diagram 773, for example, White X-rays the Queen in order to win a Rook.

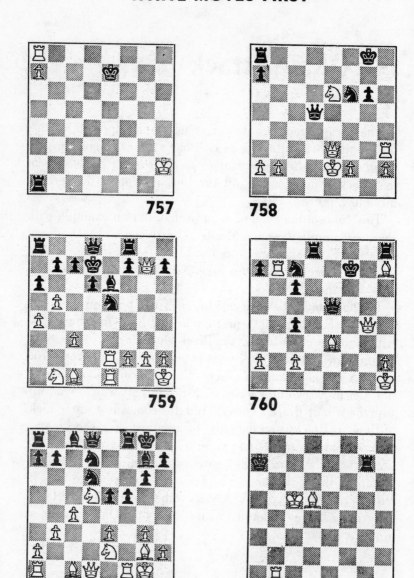

757

758

759

760

761

762

WHITE MOVES FIRST

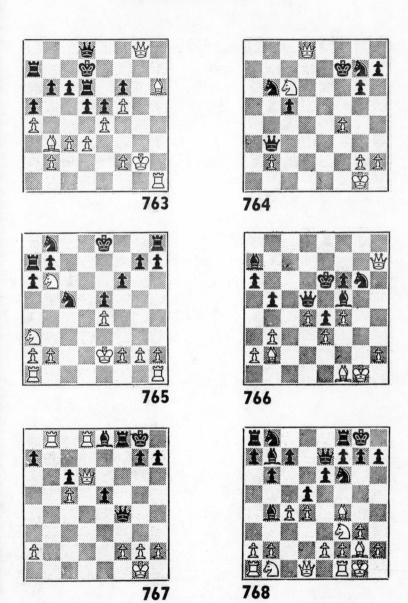

763

764

765

766

767

768

769

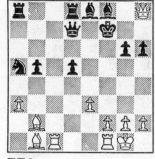

770

771

772

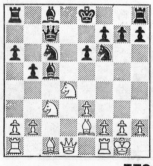

773

774

BLACK MOVES FIRST

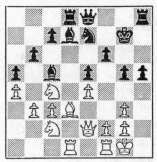

775

776

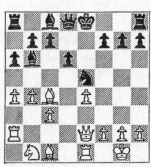

777

778

779

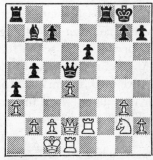

780

15. Surprise Moves

Occasionally we see moves that are so remarkable they do not fit into any systematic classification. Or even if they do, they are so astounding that their surprise value is the most impressive thing about them. Still other surprise moves are notable because they violate a standard rule!

To consider the last group first, examine Diagram 787. It is well known that a Rook is helpless against far-advanced passed Pawns, and our first impulse would be to dismiss this position as a perfect case in point. Yet White does not resign; he allows Black to queen, and then sacrifices his Rook! Suddenly it turns out that White has a mate in three! Instead of being dismayed at this violation of general principles, we are of course delighted.

In Diagram 789 we see the value of an alert and imaginative approach to the game. White is threatened with mate, and his first thought is to find a defense. But then comes the inspired N—N6ch!—attack rather than defense!—and Black can resign.

Perhaps the most surprising of surprise moves are those which come in the ending. Here the position has been so simplified that the scope for surprise seems altogether too thin. And yet masters can think up such pleasantries as the opening move in Diagram 817 which leaves Black a Rook down—with a won game! And the moral? A surprise move may be possible in *any* position.

WHITE MOVES FIRST

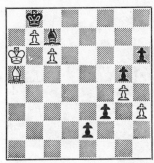

781

782

783

784

785

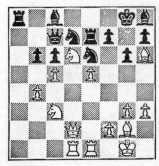

786

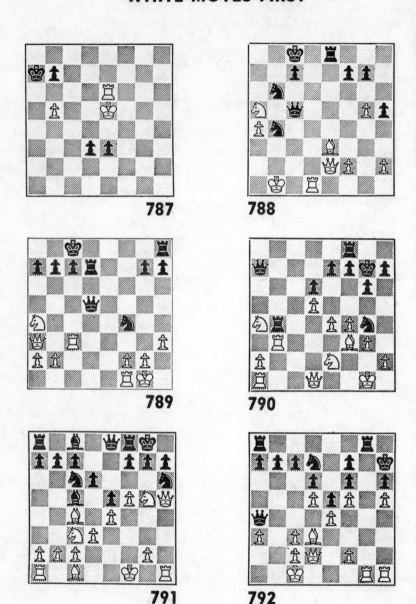

787

788

789

790

791

792

WHITE MOVES FIRST

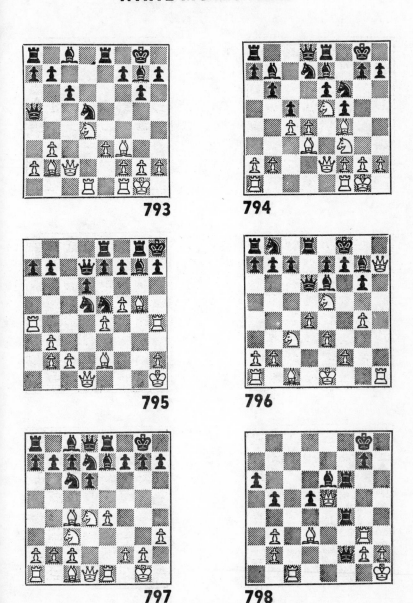

793

794

795

796

797

798

WHITE MOVES FIRST

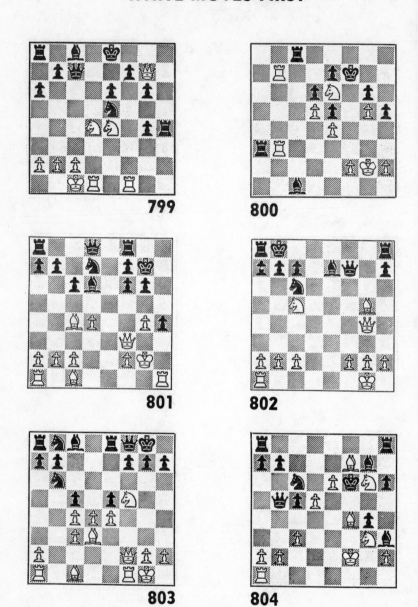

799

800

801

802

803

804

BLACK MOVES FIRST

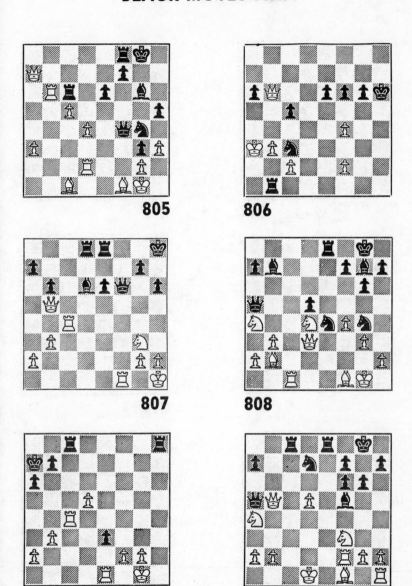

805

806

807

808

809

810

BLACK MOVES FIRST

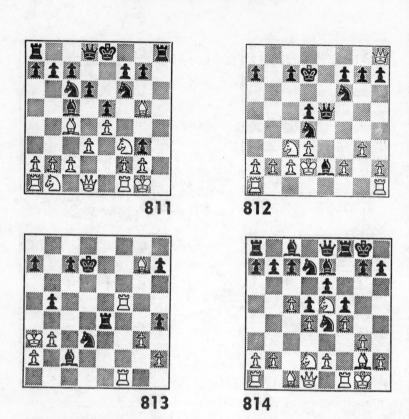

811

812

813

814

815

816

16. Defensive Combinations

This may seem a surprising subject for a book on tactical motifs. But defense is not merely passive, and in fact the best defense is never merely passive. Resourceful defense often calls for a thorough mastery of tactics. Without such mastery many a desperate position would utterly collapse.

In Diagram 824, for example, White, who is just about to lose his Queen, seems on the point of resigning. Yet he evolves a neat plan for winning Black's Queen in return. And in the last analysis this plan depends on a Knight fork.

No less ingenious is White's procedure in Diagram 827. Menaced with a mating attack, he gives up his Queen and soon demonstrates that it is Black's King, and not his own, that is fatally menaced.

In Diagram 830, too, White is threatened with mate. Yet he fights out his way out in such an ingenious manner that it is Black who gets mated.

Such examples show us the power of active, ingenious defense—really counterattack. It has been well said that counterattack is the best defense.

BLACK MOVES FIRST

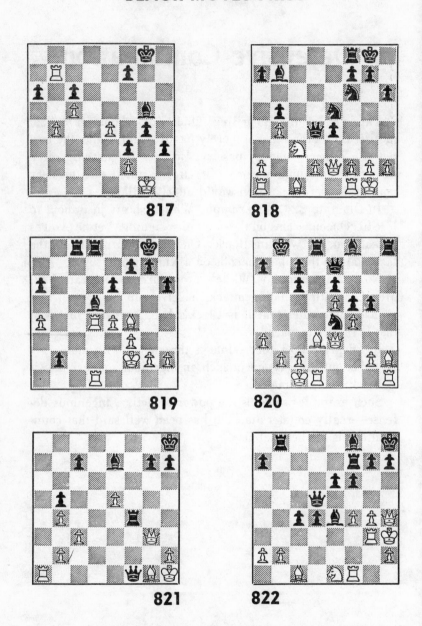

817

818

819

820

821

822

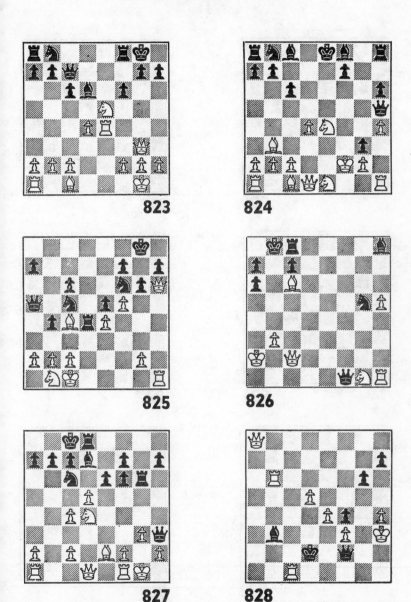

823

824

825

826

827

828

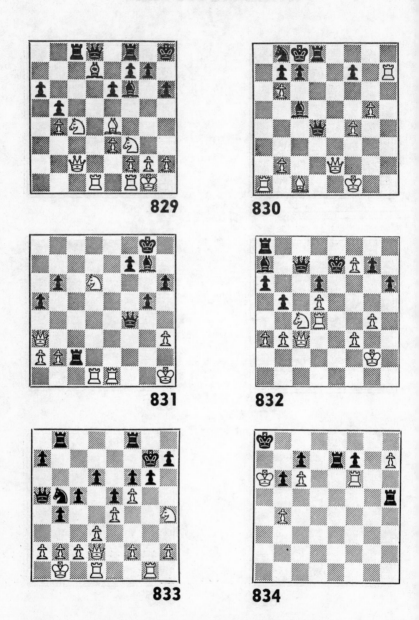

829

830

831

832

833

834

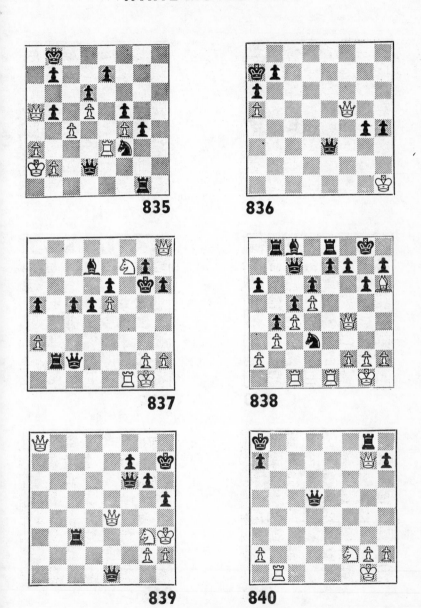

835

836

837

838

839

840

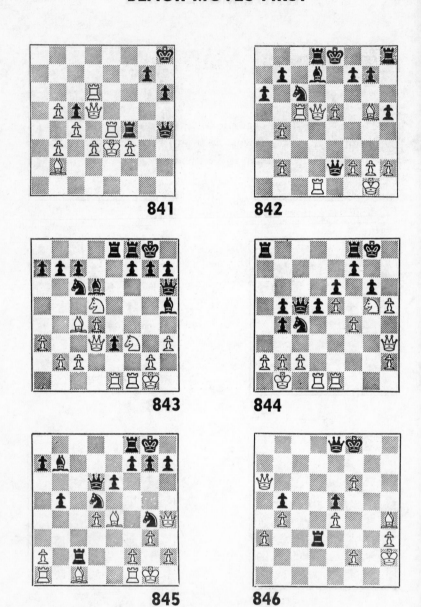

841

842

843

844

845

846

17. Trapped Man

The most common example of this theme is the trapping of a Bishop in a net of Pawns, as shown in Diagram 854. (This opening trap is so old that it is called "the Noah's Ark Trap.")

But other units can be trapped, too, and strangely enough the Queen, the mightiest of all the pieces, is particularly vulnerable to a pincer movement executed by pieces of lesser value.

That is what happens, for example, in Diagrams 847, 849, and 851. The moral is that the Queen is too valuable to be squandered on aimless expeditions without adequate support.

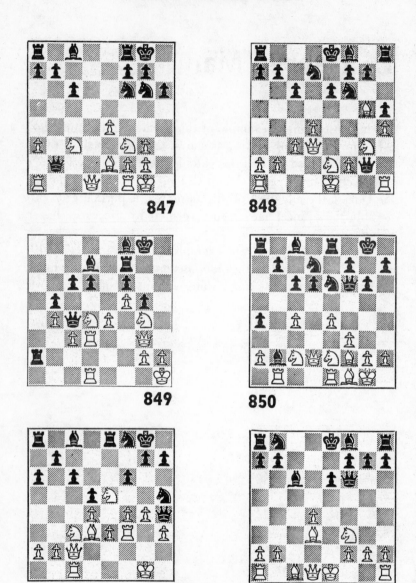

847

848

849

850

851

852

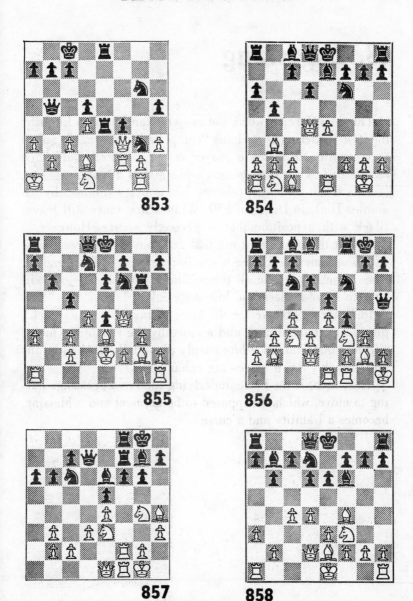

853

854

855

856

857

858

18. Zugzwang

This is a German word, not easy to translate into English; the best rendering is perhaps "compelled to move." It refers to *a position in which a player is not menaced, but which results in loss for him as soon as he makes a move.*

This is not a difficult concept, but is best explained by example. Thus, in Diagram 859, White's first move still leaves Black with a position that is perfectly secure. However, a glance at the position shows that any move of a Black *piece* will lose material. Hence Black is restricted to Pawn moves. Once Black has made all the available Pawn moves, he will have to move a piece and lose material.

In Diagram 860 we see the same picture. Some of Black's pieces are immobilized, and a move by the remaining pieces will lose material. So White simply plays 1 P—R4! and waits until Black's Pawn moves are exhausted.

This, then, is the basic underlying idea of *Zugzwang*: having to move, which is supposed to be an asset and a blessing, becomes a liability and a curse.

WHITE MOVES FIRST

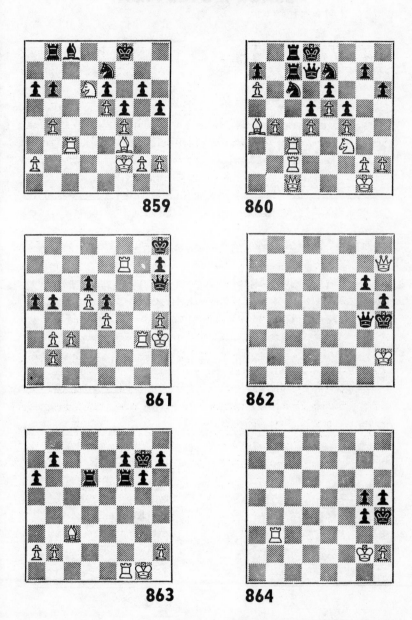

859

860

861

862

863

864

BLACK MOVES FIRST

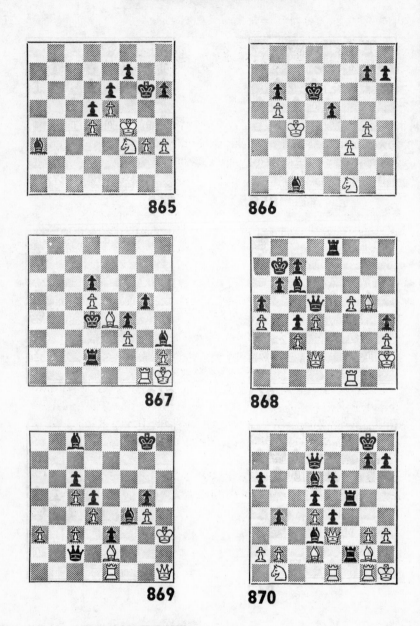

865

866

867

868

869

870

19. The Helpless King

When you are subjecting your opponent's King to a very powerful attack and he lacks adequate support by his pieces, you can make all sorts of brilliant sacrifices.

In Diagram 873, for example, Black runs into one of the most curious checkmates ever performed on the chessboard. His King is driven right down the board and mated by a castling move! Such extraordinary happenings are to be expected when a King has already been harried toward the center of the board.

In Diagram 879 the conclusion is even more picturesque. But what can Black expect with his Queen buried at Queen Rook 1, far from the scene of action? Incidentally, the absence of the defending Queen from the critical zone of attack is often the key to a brilliant combination. Diagram 885 is another case in point, and so is Diagram 889.

Even in the endgame stage, with material greatly simplified, the King may be exposed to serious tactical dangers. Thus, in Diagram 871 White drives the Black King into a mating net, while in Diagram 899 Black's King succumbs to a strikingly artistic finish.

All the examples in this section prove this point: the helpless King is a target for brilliant sacrifices and combinations.

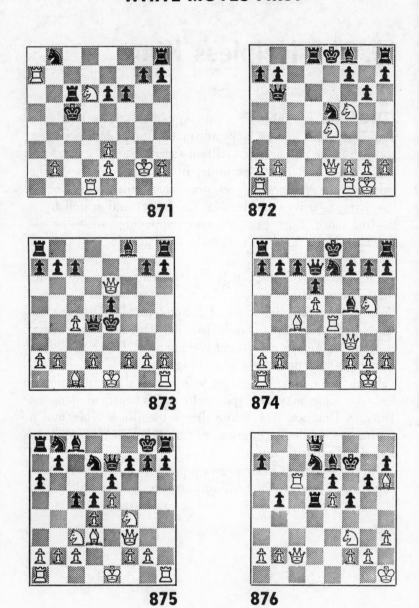

871

872

873

874

875

876

WHITE MOVES FIRST

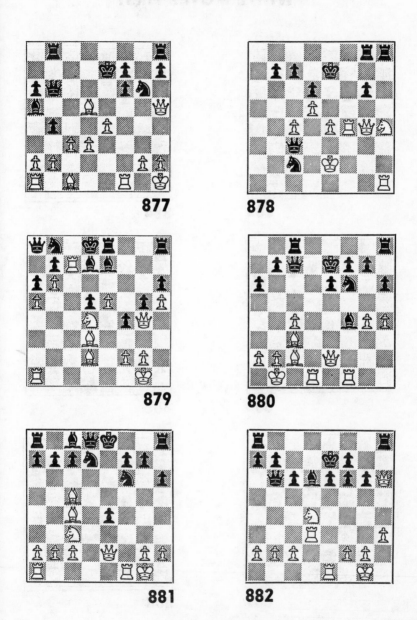

877

878

879

880

881

882

· The HELPLESS KING · 177

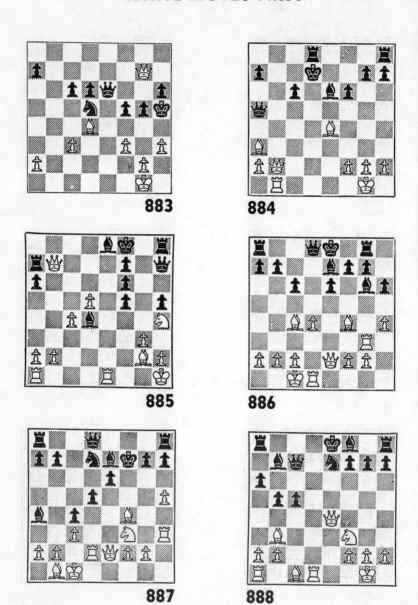

883

884

885

886

887

888

WHITE MOVES FIRST

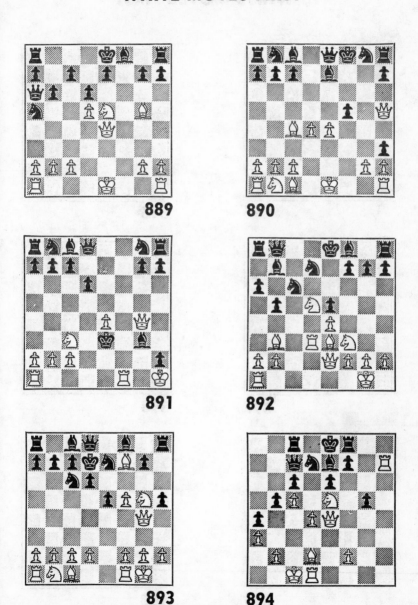

889

890

891

892

893

894

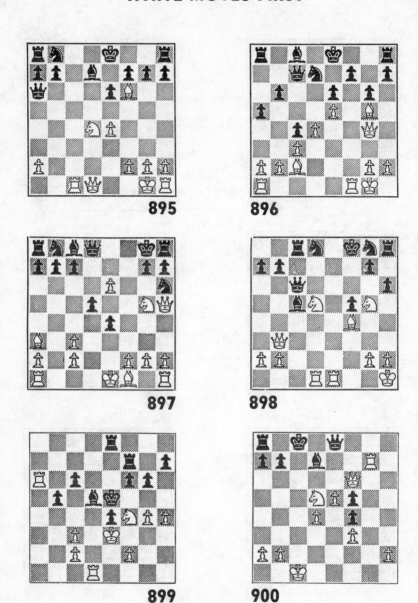

895

896

897

898

899

900

BLACK MOVES FIRST

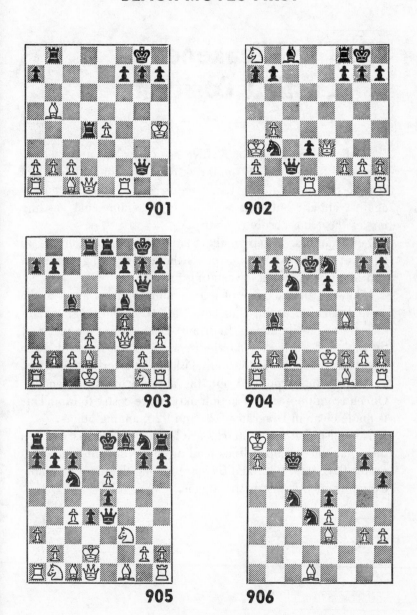

901

902

903

904

905

906

20. The Weakened Castled Position

In the previous section you've seen how the unprotected, uncastled King becomes the target of many kinds of brilliant attack. By castling, the King acquires a certain immunity against attack; but it is a mistake to assume that castling makes the King absolutely safe.

For example, a gap in the castled Pawn position (as in Diagrams 911 and 917) exposes the castled King to attack, and often brings on a devastating finish.

Likewise, the advance of one or more of the Pawns in the castled position (as in Diagrams 908, 912, and 924) creates targets for hostile attack. Brilliant sacrifices are the order of the day, and while they dazzle us, we must not forget that the positional weakness is the source of the attacker's inspiration.

As previously pointed out, the absence of the defender's Queen from the scene of action may prove costly to him. This is made clear in Diagrams 925 and 926, among others.

Note also that many attacks are brilliantly successful when they make use of open lines leading to the hostile King. Diagrams 928, 929, 932, and 941 are among the many valuable examples of this instructive theme.

WHITE MOVES FIRST

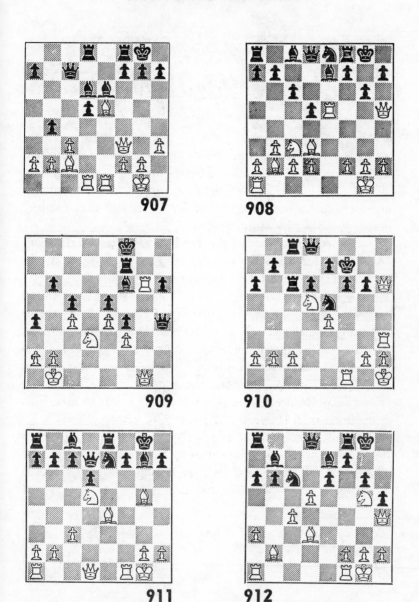

907

908

909

910

911

912

· The WEAKENED CASTLED POSITION · 183

WHITE MOVES FIRST

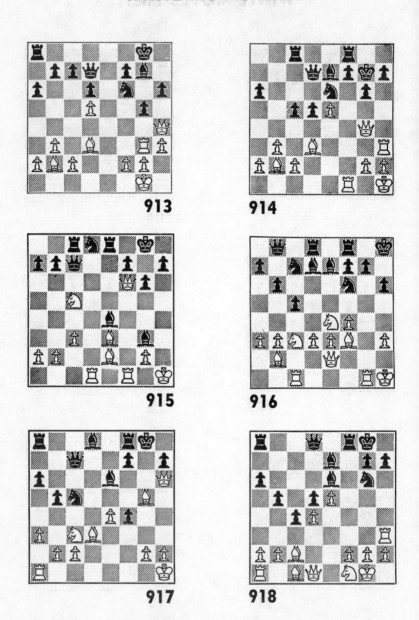

913

914

915

916

917

918

184 · The WEAKENED CASTLED POSITION ·

WHITE MOVES FIRST

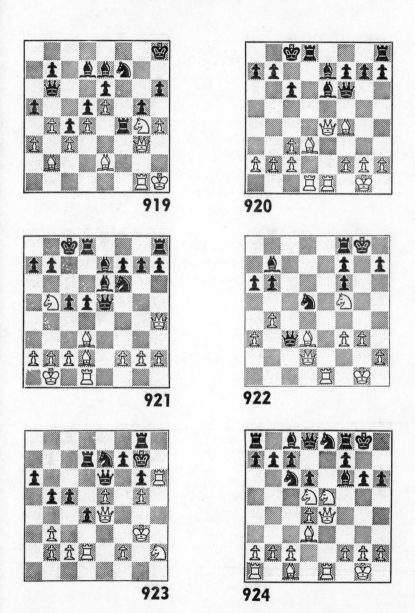

919

920

921

922

923

924

· The WEAKENED CASTLED POSITION · 185

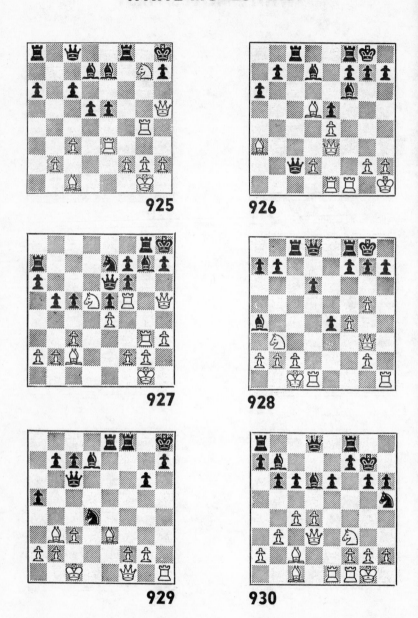

925

926

927

928

929

930

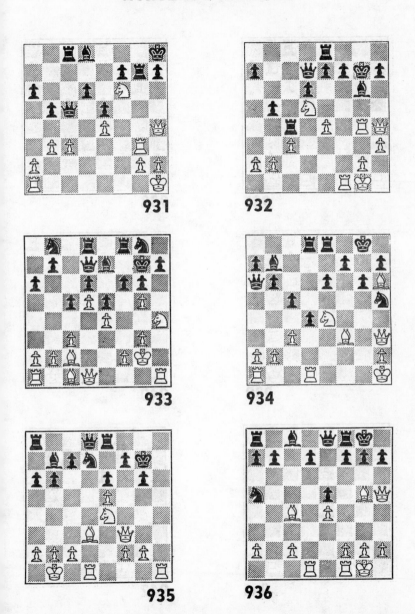

931

932

933

934

935

936

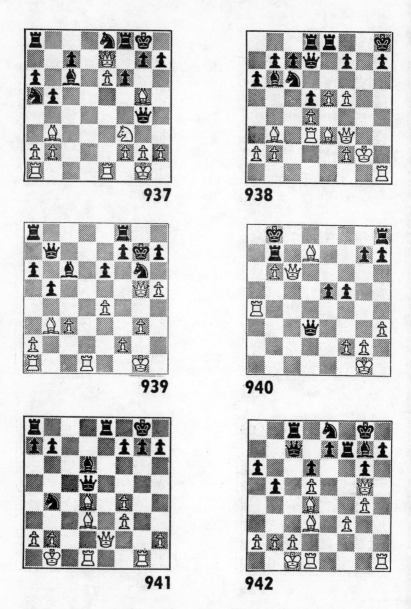

937

938

939

940

941

942

188 · The WEAKENED CASTLED POSITION ·

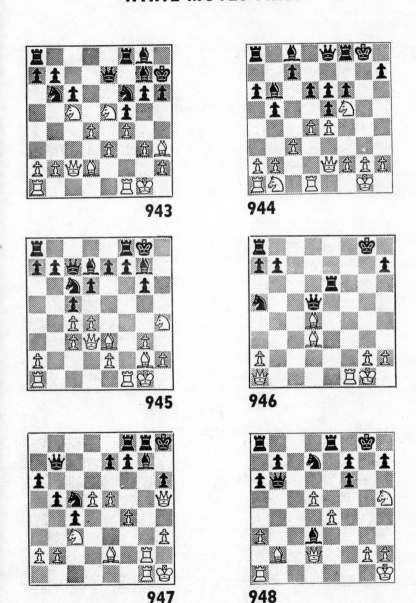

943

944

945

946

947

948

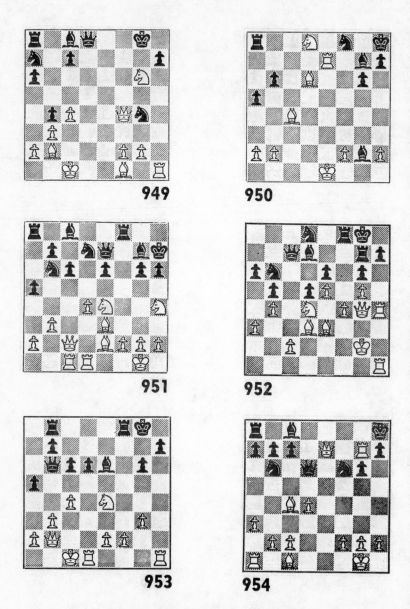

949

950

951

952

953

954

190 · The WEAKENED CASTLED POSITION ·

WHITE MOVES FIRST

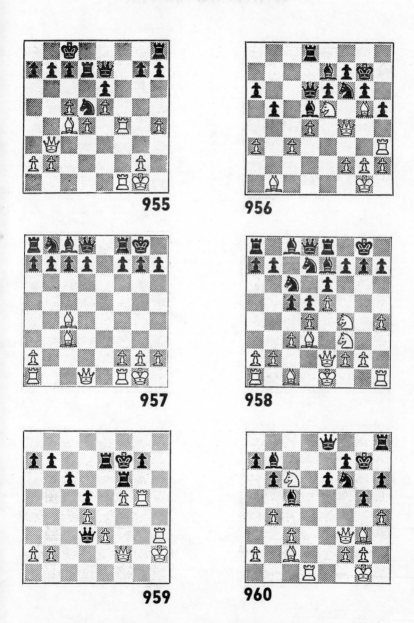

955

956

957

958

959

960

· The WEAKENED CASTLED POSITION · 191

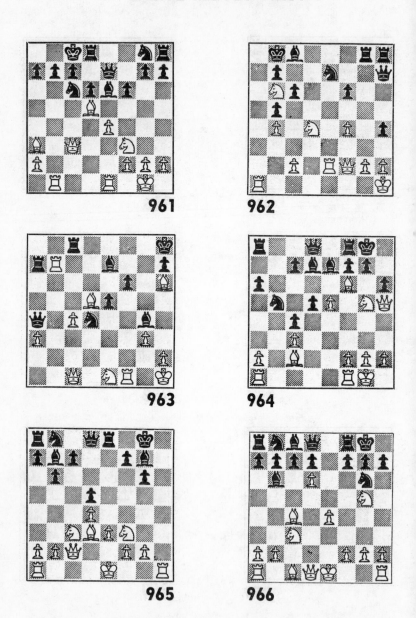

961

962

963

964

965

966

WHITE MOVES FIRST

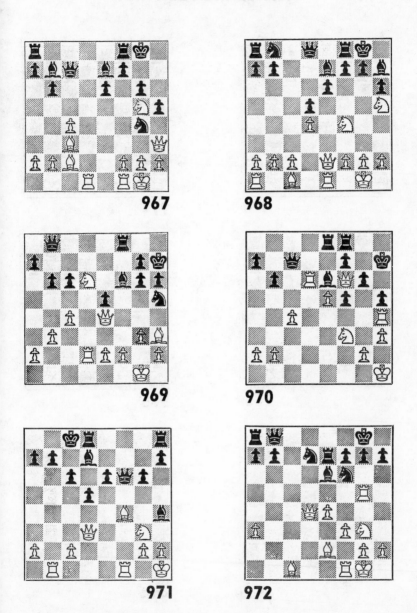

967

968

969

970

971

972

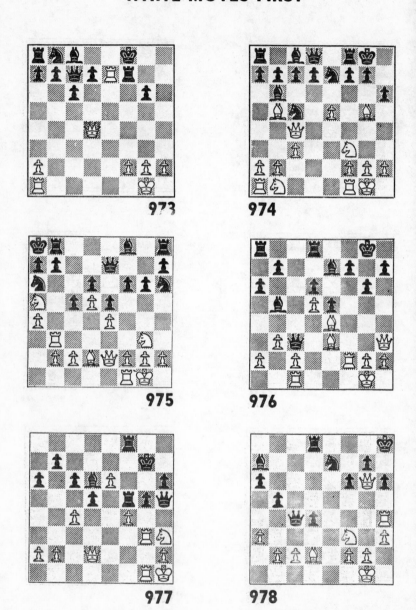

973

974

975

976

977

978

BLACK MOVES FIRST

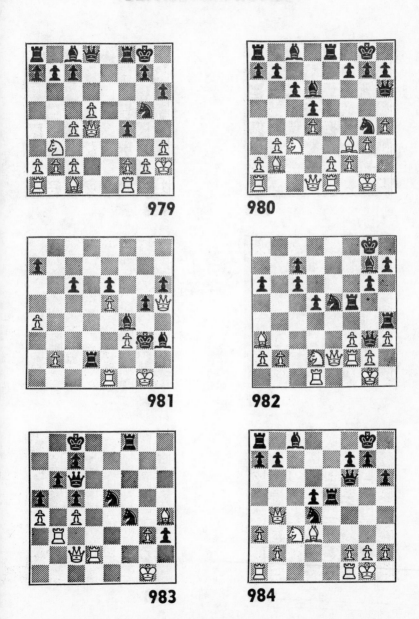

979

980

981

982

983

984

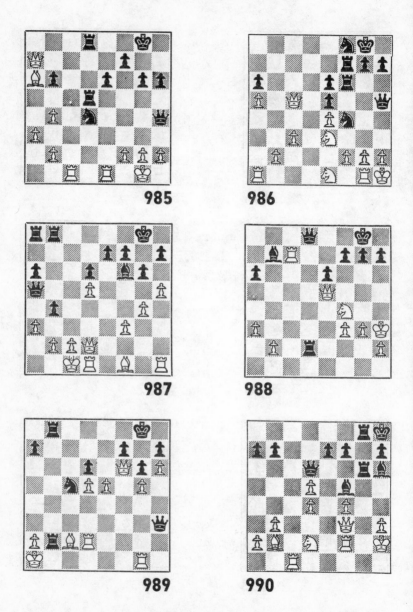

985

986

987

988

989

990

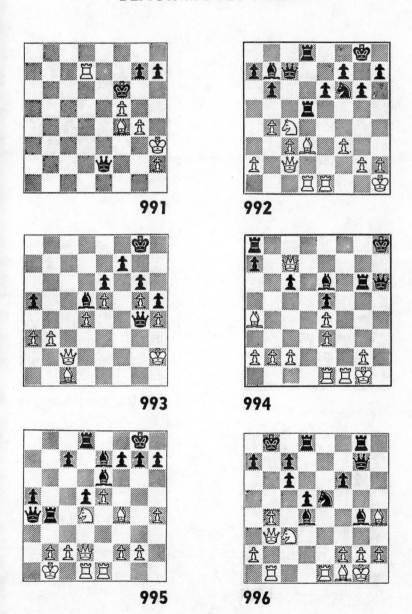

991

992

993

994

995

996

BLACK MOVES FIRST

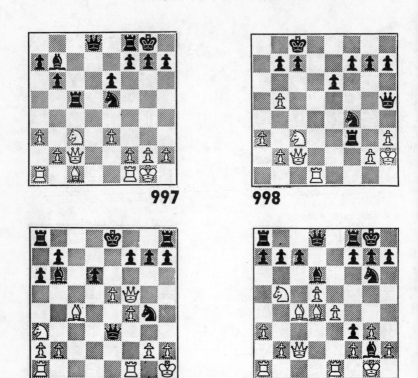

997

998

999

1000

1001

198 · The WEAKENED CASTLED POSITION ·

Solutions

1 White piles up on the pinned piece:

1 R—Q1!	QxQ
2 RxRch	K moves
3 PxQ	Resigns

2

1 R—K8!!	QxR
2 QxNch	K—N1
3 B—R6	Q—B2
4 Q—Q8ch	Q—B1
5 QxQ mate	

3

1 P—B4!	N—K2

If 1 ... NxP; 2 RxN.

2 P—B5	....

Winning the pinned piece.

4 White wins a piece:

1 BxN!	QxB
2 QxQ	PxQ
3 BxB etc.	

5

1 RxN!	PxR
2 B—R8!	Resigns

Black is helpless against the coming Q—N7 mate.

6

1 Q—R4ch!	K—N1
2 Q—N3ch!	K—R1
3 B—B3	....

White wins the Queen.

7

1 Q—N8ch!!	K—K2

If 1 . . . KxQ; 2 N—N6! followed by R—R8 mate!

2 QxBPch	K—Q1
3 N—N6	QxNP
4 R—Q1ch	B—Q2
5 QxRch!	Resigns

For if 5 ... KxQ; 6 R—R8 mate.

8 White wins a Rook:

1 B—K4!	QxQ
2 BxQ etc.	

9

1 NxB	RxN
2 BxN!	RxB
3 P—N6	....

White wins a piece.

10

1 N—Q6!	R—K2
2 N/R4xP	BxN
3 NxB	R—K3
4 B—N3 and wins	

11 White keeps the extra piece by a counter-pin:

1 Q—R8!	Resigns

12

1 N—K7ch!	QxN
2 RxQ etc.	

If 2 ... RxQ; 3 R—K8 mate.

13

1 NxBP	Q—Q2
2 N—K7ch!	QxN
3 QxR etc.	

White has won the Exchange.

14

1 Q—N7!	KR—B1

If 1 . . . Q—Q3; 2 NxN, PxN; 3 RxP etc.

2 NxP!	Q—Q3

If 2 ... PxN; 3 RxR etc.

3 RxP!!	Resigns

If 3 . . . RxR; 4 QxQRch winning more material.

15

1 N—B7ch!	R/B2xN

Not 1 . . . BxN?; 2 QxN mate.

2 PxR and wins	

Black has no defense to the coming RxB, as his King Rook Pawn is pinned.

16

1 RxN!	PxR
2 R—KN1 and wins	

17 White "piles up" on the pinned Knight and wins it:

1 B—B4 etc.	

18

1 N—Q7!!	NxN
2 QxBch	QxQ
3 BxQch	R—B2
4 BxRch and wins	

19

1 R—KN4!	Resigns

If 1 . . . QxR; 2 QxPch and 3 QxP mate.

20

1 BxN!	Resigns

If 1 . . . PxB; 2 RxQ; or 1 . . . BxB; 2 QxBPch winning.

21

1 RxPch!!	KxR
2 R—N1 and wins	

22

1 BxP!	QxB
2 R—B7	R—K2
3 RxR	QxR
4 R—B7	Resigns

23　　1 N—B7ch　　　K—N1
　　　　2 N—Q6 dis ch Q—K3
　　　　3 R—K1!! and wins
　　If 3 . . . QxQ; 4 RxR mate.

24　　1 Q—KN1!　　　R—K1
　　White threatened mate.
　　　　2 B—R5!　　　R—Q1
　　　　3 Q—R2　　　Resigns
　　The Knight is lost.

25　　1 P—N4ch!　　　KxP
　　　　2 B—K6 and wins

26　　1 RxB!　　　RxR
　　　　2 R—KB1　　QR—KB1
　　　　3 Q—N5　　　K—N2
　　　　4 RxR　　　RxR
　　　　5 BxRch　　　QxB
　　　　6 N—R5ch　　　. . . .
　　White wins the Queen.

27　　1 PxPch　　　BxP
　　　　2 RxB!　　　RxR
　　　　3 R—KB1　　　R—B1
　　　　4 R—B3!　　R/B1—B3
　　　　5 K—B2! and wins
　　White wins the pinned piece by 6
　　K—N3 and 7 K—N4.

28　　1 N—B7!　　　QxN
　　　　2 QxR　　　. . . .
　　White has won the Exchange.

29　　1 B—N5!　　　PxB
　　　　2 PxP　　　. . . .
　　Black must save his Queen, allow-
　　ing White's 3 RxR.

30　　1 R—QN3!　　　PxR
　　If Black's Queen retreats, White
　　has a winning attack.
　　　　2 QxQ and wins
　　Black's Bishop Pawn is pinned!

31　　1 NxN!!　　　BxQ
　　　　2 B—N5ch　　P—QB3
　　　　3 PxP and wins
　　The double threat of 4 PxP dis ch
　　and 4 P—B7 dis ch is decisive.

32　　1 NxP!　　　NxN
　　　　2 Q—N4! and wins
　　The double threat of 3 QxNch
　　and 3 QxBch is too strong.

33　　1 BxN!　　　BxB
　　Or 1 . . . PxB; 2 N—K5 with a
　　winning pin on the open file.
　　　　2 RxQch and wins

34　　1 NxKP!　　　Resigns
　　White wins the Queen, as 1 . . .
　　PxN allows 2 Q—Q8 mate.

35　　1 NxKPch!　　　PxN
　　　　2 RxPch!　　　Resigns
　　If 2 . . . PxR; 3 Q—N8 mate. If
　　2 . . . K—K1; 3 RxP wins easily.

36　　1 N—K7ch!　　　Resigns
　　If 1 . . . QxN; 2 QxBch, Q—B1;
　　3 B—R7ch wins the Queen.

37　　1 BxPch!　　　RxB
　　　　2 RxN/K4!　　　QxR
　　　　3 QxRch　　　K—R1
　　　　4 N/B3—K4!　　　. . . .
　　If now 4 . . . B—Q5; 5 BxB, QxB;
　　6 QxRch! forces mate. And if 4 . . .
　　Q—K2; 5 RxN! etc.
　　　　4 . . . .　　　QxB
　　　　5 NxN　　　Q—K7
　　　　6 Q—N8ch!　　　RxQ
　　　　7 N—B7 mate

38　　1 NxNP!!　　　BxN
　　　　2 RxB!　　　RxR
　　　　3 BxP　　　NxBP
　　　　4 RxR!　　　QxR
　　If 4 . . . NxQ; 5 RxQ dis ch,
　　K—R1; 6 RxR and wins.
　　　　5 BxQch　　　KxB
　　　　6 Q—N4ch　　　Resigns

39　　1 P—K5!　　　BxP
　　　　2 NxB　　　QxN
　　　　3 R—K1　　　N—K5
　　　　4 P—KB3 and wins

40　　1 NxN　　　BxN
　　　　2 N—R5ch!　　　PxN
　　　　3 Q—N5ch!　　　K—R1
　　　　4 BxBch　　　. . . .
　　White wins the Queen.

41　　1 B—N1!　　　. . . .
　　Threatens 2 BxN and 3 QxP mate.
　　　　1 . . . .　　　P—N3
　　　　2 BxN!　　　BxB
　　　　3 N—K4!　　　Resigns
　　For after 3 . . . B—K2; 4 P—
　　QN4 wins the pinned Knight.

42　　Black threatens to break out of
　　the pin with . . . N—B6ch. But
　　White is alert:
　　　　1 K—B1!　　　K—N2
　　　　2 R—B2　　　K—B3
　　　　3 R/B2—K2　　P—KR4
　　　　4 RxN　　　Resigns

43	1 P—K5!	PxP
	2 NxB	KxN
	3 B—N5	B—B4
	4 NxBch	PxN
	5 QxP	Q—Q3
	6 R—Q1!	Q—K3
	7 BxNch	Resigns

If 1 . . . QxB; 8 R—Q7ch wins.

44 1 NxP! B—QB2
If 1 . . . NxN??; 2 Q—K8 mate;
and on 1 . . . PxN; 2 QxB wins.
2 N—Q5! Resigns
If 2 . . . BxN; 3 N—Q7ch wins
the Queen. If 2 . . . QxB; 3 NxB
attacks the Queen and threatens 4
Q—K8 mate.

45 White has a slow win with 1
NxQ, RxRch; 2 KxR, BxQ; 3 NxP
etc. Much faster is:
1 B—QR3! BxN
Or 1 . . . QxB; 2 QxP mate.
2 BxQch and wins

46 1 P—B6! RxP!
If now 2 RxR? Black is stalemated!
2 P—B7! R—QB3
3 R—R6! Resigns
If 3 . . . RxR; 4 P—B8/Q mate.

47 1 P—Q5!! PxP
2 NxN Q—Q2
If 2 . . . BxN; 3 QxBch wins.
3 N—R5! Resigns
The double threat of 4 NxB and
4 BxP decides.

48 1 R—K6! Resigns
If 1 . . . PxR; 2 QxPch, K—R1;
3 BxNch and 4 Q—R7 mate.

49 1 RxN! RxR
2 R—Q1 Q—K3
3 BxRch NxB
4 Q—N8ch! NxQ
5 R—Q8 mate

50 1 P—KN4! Resigns
If Black moves the attacked
Knight, he loses the other Knight.
And if 1 . . . PxP; 2 NxP/N4 win-
ning the pinned Knight.

51 1 B—B5! K—B1
2 Q—B6! Resigns
White wins the miserable Bishop.

52 1 Q—B4! N—K3
2 Q—QR4ch! Q—B3
3 B—QN5 ....
White wins the Queen.

53 1 B—N5!! RxB
2 QR—Q1 Q—B1
3 Q—K3! and wins
White's mating threat forces 3 . . .
Castles, and after 4 QxR White is
the Exchange ahead.

54 1 Q—K3! Q—N1
If 1 . . . Q—Q3; 2 N—B6ch wins
Black's Queen. If 1 . . . BxN; 2 RxB,
N—Q2; 3 Q—Q4 wins the pinned
Knight.
2 R—K1 BxN
3 BxBch N—B2
4 R—KB1 Resigns
White wins the pinned Knight.

55 1 N—B5!! PxN
2 B—B4!! B—Q3
If 2 . . . QxB; 3 Q—B8ch, K—K2;
4 QxR wins. If 2 . . . Q—Q1; 3
QxR etc. wins.
3 BxB R—N3
4 QxNch! Resigns
White comes out a piece up.

56 1 P—B6! B—N5
If 1 . . . PxP; 2 Q—N6ch fol-
lowed by 3 Q—R7 mate.
2 Q—N6! Resigns
White forces 3 QxNP mate or 3
Q—R7 mate.

57 1 BxN! BxB
Or 1 . . . PxB; 2 Q—N4ch, K—
R1; 3 NxPch winning the Exchange.
2 QxPch!! KxQ
3 R—R5ch K—N1
4 N—N6! Resigns
For 5 R—R8 mate follows.

58 1 P—B5! P—K5
The Bishop is helpless.
2 PxB! PxN
3 P—Q7! Resigns
White attacks Knight and Rook.

59 1 NxN!! Q—R4ch
Or 1 . . . BxQ; 2 B—N5ch, Q—
Q2; 3 BxQch, K—Q1; 4 NxPch,
KxB; 5 KxB and White has won too
much material.
2 B—Q2 BxQ
3 BxQ PxN
4 B—N5 mate!

60   1 Q—B6 mate

61   1 B—Q4!   P—K4
       2 BxP!   QxB
       3 Q—R6 mate

62   1 RxB!   QxR
       2 Q—B3   K—N2
If 2 . . . B—B4; 3 NxB, PxN; 4
Q—N3!, K—N2; 5 BxN dbl ch,
KxB; 6 Q—R4ch!, K—K3; 7 R—
K1ch winning.
       3 N/B3—K4!!   PxN
       4 NxP   Q—K3
Or 4 . . . QxN; 5 QxNch, K—N1;
6 B—R6 followed by mate.
       5 BxNch   K—N1
       6 Q—B4   Resigns
For 7 Q—R6 wins.

63   1 R—K1!!   RxP
If 1 . . . BxB; 2 QxQ wins.
       2 BxBch   QxB
       3 Q—R7ch   B—N2
       4 QxPch   Resigns
White wins on material.

64   1 B—B4   Resigns

65   1 BxNch   PxB
       2 NxP!!   Resigns
If 2 . . . RxQch; 3 RxR and
Black's Queen is trapped because of
the mate threat (3 . . . Q—K3??;
4 R—Q8 mate). After 3 . . . Q—Q2;
4 RxQ, KxR; 5 NxP White wins
easily.

66   1 QxPch!!   KxQ
       2 R—KR5 mate

67   1 QxN!!   PxQ
Or 1 . . . BxR; 2 RxB! with material plus.
       2 BxPch   K—R1
       3 N—N6ch   K—R2
       4 NxR dbl ch   K—R1
       5 N—N6ch   K—R2
       6 N—K5 disch! K—R1
       7 N—B7 mate

68   1 RxR   PxR
       2 P—K6!   QxQ
       3 NxQ   . . . .
White wins the Bishop.

69   1 R—N3!   PxR
       2 BxQ and wins

70   1 RxN!!   PxR
       2 N—K6ch!!   PxN
       3 R—B7ch   Resigns
White continues 4 QxQ.

71   1 NxP!   QNxN
       2 RxN!   NxR
       3 RxN!   QxR
       4 N—N5!!   Q—N3
If 4 . . . QxQ; 5 N—B7 mate!
       5 QxPch!!   QxQ
       6 N—B7 mate

72   1 N—N6!   Resigns
White wins the Queen!

73   1 . . . .   QxPch!
       2 QxQ   RxR
       Resigns

74   1 . . . .   P—Q5!!
       2 QxP   Q—R8ch
This wins White's Knight (after
3 Q—Q1 etc.) as 3 N—Q1?? allows
3 . . . QxQ.

75   1 . . . .   RxPch!!
       2 BxR   QxBch etc.
Black's counter-pin wins for him!

76   1 . . . .   B—R3!!
       2 P—KN5   BxP!
       3 P—B4   BxP!
       4 B—K3   BxB
       5 QxB   QxBP mate

77   1 . . . .   N—N6ch!
       2 PxN   Q—R6ch
       3 K—N1   BxBch
       Resigns
If 4 QxB or 4 R—B2 Black has
4 . . . QxP/N7 mate.

78   1 . . . .   R/B1—B6!
       2 Q—K2   B—N4!
If now 3 BxB, RxB wins a piece
for Black.
       3 R/B1—Q1   Q—B2!
       4 B—Q4   RxB!
       5 RxR   Q—B5!
       Resigns
Black comes out a piece to the
good.

79   1 . . . .   Q—N3!
If now 2 N/B3—K2, Black wins a
piece by 2 . . . P—K4.
       2 B—K3   P—K4
       3 N—R4   Q—R2!
Black must win a piece.

80	1	N—K5!!

If now 2 BxQ, BxP mate!

	2 B—K3	BxB
	3 PxB	Q—R5ch
	4 P—KN3	NxNP

Black has a winning game.

81	1	Q—B4!!
	2 N—B3	KR—K1!
	3 R—K1	RxB!
	4 NxR	R—K1
	5 P—KN4	RxN!!
	Resigns	

If 6 PxQ, RxR mate.

82	1	N—B6

White has nothing better than 2 NxN, RxR leaving him with a lost game.

83	1	RxPch!
	2 K—Q1	RxBch!
	Resigns	

For after 3 KxR Black exploits the new pin decisively with 3 . . . N—K5ch etc.

84	1	N/B5xQP!
	2 PxN	NxQP
	3 R—B4	B—N4!

By winning the Rook, Black undermines White's advanced Bishop.

	4 Q—K4	BxR
	5 RxB	RxB
		and wins

85	1	R/K1xN!
	2 PxR	Q—R5
	3 BxP	RxB
	4 N—K2	BxN
	5 RxR	N—N6ch!
	6 K—N1	B—B4ch
	7 R—B2	Q—B5
	Resigns	

86	1	NxNP!

If 2 BxN, Q—R5ch etc.

| | 2 Q—K2 | Q—R5ch |
| | Resigns | |

For if 3 B—B2, NxB; 4 QxN, QxQch; 5 KxQ, B—N5 and the pin wins a piece. Or 3 K—Q1, NxBch; 4 QxN, RxB!; 5 QxR, B—N5 with an even more disastrous pin.

87	1	P—Q5!

If now 2 QxP, QxBP mate!

| | 2 PxP | B—N5! |

This wins the Queen, for if 3 QxB, QxBP mate!

88	1	RxN!
	Resigns	

If 2 QPxR, Q—Q8 mate.

89	1	N—B6ch!
	2 QxN	wins

If 2 K—N2, NxRch wins the Exchange, while if 2 K—R1, NxR!; 3 QxQ?, R—B8 mate!

| | 2 .... | QxRch! |

Black comes out the Exchange ahead.

90	1	R—K8!
	2 QxR	NxBch

And Black wins the Queen.

91	1	R—R3ch!
	2 K—N1	R—R8ch!!
	3 KxR	Q—R6ch
	4 K—N1	QxP/N7 mate

92	1	PxB!
	2 RxQ	R—B8ch
	3 K—N2	R/B4—B7 mate

93	1	BxP!
	2 RxR	....

Even better for Black is 2 QxB, RxR etc.

| | 2 .... | B—B3 dis ch! |
| | | and wins |

94	1	BxBch
	2 NxB	Q—N3!
	3 QxP	NxP!

This wins, for after 4 Q—Q7, N—Q3! or 4 Q—K5, R—K3! the White Knight is lost.

95	1	BxPch!

If now 2 KxB?, QxQ wins.

| | 2 K—B1 | BxR and wins |

96	1	RxP!

If now 2 R—R3, R/Q5—Q8 wins the Knight "to begin with."

| | 2 RxR | BxR |

White is helpless against 3 . . . R—B7 winning his Rook.

97	1	K—R2!
	2 B—K1	K—R3!
	3 B—B3	K—R4!
	4 B—K1	K—N5!
	5 B—B3	PxPch
	6 RxPch	K—R6!
	7 any	BxR mate

98 1 ....   QxRch!
    2 KxQ   PxQ
    Resigns

99 1 ....   B—N4!
    2 P—B4   BxP!
    3 QxB   QxP mate

100 1 ....   RxN!
    2 QxR   NxKP
    Threatens . . . N—N6 mate or . . .
N—B7 mate, aside from attacking
White's Queen. So:
    3 Q—N2   N—B7 mate!

101 1 ....   RxB!
    2 RxR   Q—QN2!
    3 Q—KN2 Q—N8ch!
    But not 3 . . . N—B5?; 4 R—
Q8ch!
    4 Q—N1   Q—K5ch!
    5 Q—N2   QxQch
    6 KxQ   N—B5ch
    Black wins the Rook and remains
a piece ahead.

102 1 ....   R—N5!!
    Resigns
    For if 2 BxR, QxR/B8 mate!

103 1 ....   B—N5!
    2 QxB   NxPch
    Winning White's Queen.

104 1 ....   RxP!!
    2 QxR   Q—R4ch!
    3 R—R3   Q—K4ch
    4 K—R1   Q—K8ch
    5 K—R2   Q—KN8 mate

105 1 ....   P—R5!
    2 N—B1   P—R6!
    Black wins the Bishop.

106 1 ....   NxP!
    2 PxN   RxPch!!
    3 QxR   RxN mate

107 Black gets nowhere with . . .
PxN. Instead, by playing 1 . . . Q—
K2 he pins and wins the Knight.
Another way is 1 . . . R—K3 and if
2 Q—KB2, Q—K2; 3 N—Q2, R—
K7 etc.

108 1 ....   QxR!
    2 NxQ   BxQ
    Resigns

109 1 QxN!   QxQ
    2 NxBch   K—R1
    3 NxQ and wins

110 1 N—Q6ch   K—B1
    Black loses his Queen after 1 . . .
BxN?
    2 NxB and wins

111 1 BxB   KxB
    2 BxN   KxB
    3 N—Q6ch and wins
    After 4 NxR White is a Rook
ahead.

112 1 N—Q6ch   BxN
    2 NxBch   K moves
    3 NxBP and wins
    White will be the Exchange and
a Pawn ahead.

113 White wins the Queen:
    1 RxRch   RxR
    2 RxRch   QxR
    3 NxPch   Resigns

114 1 N—B7ch!   K—K2
    If 1 . . . RxN; 2 RxRch with the
Exchange ahead.
    2 RxR   RxR
    3 RxR   KxR
    4 N—K6ch and wins
    White's next is 5 NxB.

115 1 N—Q5!   QxBP
    If 1 . . . PxN; 2 Q—B7ch and 3
QxNP mate. If 1 . . . Q—R3; 2
Q—N4, P—QN3; 3 NxP and wins
(or 2 . . . P—N4; 3 Q—R5 and
wins).
    2 RxNPch!   KxR
    3 Q—N4ch   K—B1
    Or 3 . . . K—R1; 4 N—B7 mate.
    4 N—K7ch   ....
    The fork wins the Queen.

116 1 N—Q6   B—Q2
    White threatened N—B5ch as
well as NxB.
    2 R—K7ch   K—B3
    3 RxB   K—K3
    4 R—Q8   K—K2
    5 N—B5ch and wins

117 1 Q—R8ch!   K—R2
    2 N—B3 and wins
    White wins the Exchange.

118
1 QxQ   BxQ
2 RxR   RxR
3 N—B7ch and wins

119
1 NxQP!   BxN
White was threatening NxQ in addition to Q—R8 mate.
2 N—Q7ch and wins
White wins the Queen. (1 N—Q7ch also wins, but less simply.)

120
1 RxN!   QxR
2 QxRch!   KxQ
3 N—N6ch and wins
White will be a piece ahead.

121
After 1 PxR/Q, RxQch Black can still fight on. So:
1 PxR/N!   RxQch
2 NxRch   K moves
3 NxB and wins

122
1 N—R7!   ....
Black must move his Queen, allowing 2 NxR. If instead 1 . . . KxN; 2 QxPch and 3 Q—R7 mate.

123
1 N—N5ch   K—N1
2 Q—R7ch   K—B1
3 N—Q6ch   ....
White wins the Queen.

124
1 N—N6ch!   PxN
2 B—K6   ....
White wins the Queen.

125
1 R—R5ch!   K—B3
If 1 . . . BxR; 2 N—K6ch wins the Queen.
2 RxPch   ....
White wins the Knight.

126
1 N—Q5ch   Resigns
White wins the Rook.

127
1 NxKP!   Resigns
If 1 . . . BxN; 2 R—N8 mate. If 1 . . . PxN; 2 RxQ wins. If the Knight is not captured, White wins a Rook.

128
1 N—Q8ch!   RxN
2 QxKPch   Resigns
Black is lost after 3 QxRch.

129
1 QxB!   RxQ
2 N—Q7ch   K moves
3 NxQ   ....
White has won a piece.

130
1 NxBP!   BxN
2 N—K7ch   K moves
3 NxB and wins
White will be the Exchange and a Pawn ahead.

131
1 P—N4!   B—N3
2 P—N5   N—R4
3 N—K7ch   ....
White wins the Queen.

132
The immediate QxR will not do because of . . . QxRch. Therefore:
1 N—B7ch!   K—N1
If 1 . . . RxN; 2 Q—B8ch leads to mate.
2 N—R6ch   K—R1
3 QxPch!!   KxQ
4 NxRch and wins

133
1 NxPch!   PxN
2 RxPch   Resigns

134
1 RxPch!   QxR
2 N—K7ch   Resigns
White wins the Queen.

135
1 N—B6ch!   BxN
2 QxPch   any
3 Q—R7 mate

136
1 N—B6ch!   PxN
2 Q—KN3ch   Resigns
If 2 . . . B—N2; 3 BxP etc.

137
1 N—Q6ch!   BxN
2 RxNch   B—K2
3 RxBch!   KxR
4 N—B6ch   Resigns
After 5 NxR White will be a piece ahead.

138
1 RxN!   QxR
2 R—Q8!   QxR
On 2 . . . Q—K2 or the like, White has 3 R—KR8 mate.
3 NxPch   K moves
4 NxQ and wins

139
1 P—N5ch!   Resigns
If Black takes either Knight, 2 N—Q7ch wins the Rook. If 1 . . . K—B2; 2 N—K6ch with the same result.

140
1 N—B6ch   BxN
2 PxB   Resigns
The coming check on the King file leaves Black helpless.

141 1 Q—B6!   QxQ
     2 NxQ   ....
White threatens RxN and also
NxR and N—Q7ch.
     2 ....   N—B6
     3 R—B4   N—Q7ch
     4 K—R2   NxB
     5 KxN!   R—R1
     6 N—Q7ch and wins
With the Exchange ahead, White
will have an easy win.

142 1 RxPch!!   K—N1
If 1 ... KxR; 2 N—N5ch! QxN;
3 Q—K6ch, K—B1; 4 QxN mate or
2 ... K—N1; 3 Q—K6ch, K—R1;
4 N—B7ch winning the Queen.
     2 N—N5!   N—B3
If 2 . . . QxN; 3 RxNch, KxR;
4 Q—K6 mate.
     3 RxBch   Resigns
If 3 ... KxR; 4 N—K6ch wins
the Queen.

143 1 QxR!   BPxQ
     2 N—B7ch and wins
After 3 NxR White will be the
Exchange ahead.

144 1 QxN!   RxQ
     2 N—B6ch   K—K2
     3 NxRch!   K—K1
     4 N—B6ch   K—K2
     5 NxQ and wins
White is the Exchange ahead.

145 1 RxP!   BxR
     2 Q—B3!!   ....
White threatens 3 QxBch and 4
Q—K7 mate. If now 2 . . . Q—K3;
3 NxPch or if 2 . . . Q—Q2; 3
N—B6ch winning the Queen. Also
if 2 ... B—N1; 3 Q—B8ch, K—Q2;
4 Q—N7ch, K—B3; 5 N—K7ch
with the same result.
     2 ....   BxN
     3 BPxB!   Resigns
White's mate threat decides.

146 1 QxRch!   RxQ
     2 N—K6ch and wins
After 3 NxQ White is a piece
ahead.

147 1 R—K8!!   Q—N4
If 1 ... QxR; 2 N—R5ch, K—
R2; 3 N—B6ch wins.
     2 Q—K3   ....
Threatens 3 R—K7ch, K—B3; 4
Q—K5 mate.
     2 ....   P—KR4
     3 Q—K5ch   Resigns
If 3 ... Q—B3; 4 R—K7ch wins
the Queen.

148 1 N—N6!!   PxN
     2 PxP   R—B3
If 2 . . . N—B3; 3 Q—R2 forces
mate.
     3 R—R8ch!   Resigns
If 3 ... KxR; 4 Q—R2ch, K—
N1; 5 Q—R7ch, K—B1; 6 Q—R8
mate.

149 1 QxB!!   PxQ
     2 NxNch   K—R1
     3 RxRch   RxR
     4 B—N7ch!   KxB
     5 NxRch   K moves
     6 NxQ and wins
White is a piece ahead.

150 1 RxB!   PxR
     2 BxP!   QxB
     3 NxBPch!   Resigns
White wins the Queen.

151 1 ....   N/K7—Q5ch!
     2 PxN   NxPch
     3 K moves   NxB etc.

152 1 ....   N—R6ch
     2 K—N2   N—N4
     Resigns
Black wins a piece.

153 1 ....   N—B5ch!
     2 PxN   R—K1ch
     Resigns
If 3 K—Q2, Q—Q6 mate. Or 3
N—K4, RxNch winning the Queen.

154 1 ....   QxR!
     2 NxQ   N—K7ch
Followed by 3 . . . NxQ and
Black has won the Exchange.

155 1 ....   N/N4—B6ch!
     2 PxN   B—R5!
     3 Q—N2   BxR
Black has won the Exchange.

156 1 ....   QxR!
     2 NxQ   N—K7ch
     Resigns
Black comes out a Rook ahead.

157 1 ....   R—Q7!
If now 2 QxR, N—B6ch wins the Queen.
    2 Q—B1   N—B6ch
If now 3 K—R1, RxP mate.
    3 K—B1   Q—N4ch
Or 3 . . . Q—R3ch with the same effect. Black mates next move.

158 1 ....   P—Q7ch!
    2 KxP   NxNch
    3 K moves   NxB
Black wins easily.

159 1 ....   NxR!
    2 NxQ   N—K7ch
    3 K—R1   NxQ
Black is a Rook ahead.

160 1 ....   P—QN4!
If now 2 B—N3, P—R5 wins the Bishop.
    2 BxNP   N—Q5ch
    3 NxN   NxNch
Followed by . . . NxB and wins.

161 1 ....   RxN!
    2 BxR   N—B4ch
    3 K moves   NxB and wins

162 1 ....   R—B8ch!
    2 RxR   RxRch
    3 KxR   N—N6ch
    4 K moves   NxQ and wins

163 1 ....   QxB!
    2 QxQ   N—B6ch
    3 K moves   NxQ and wins

164 1 ....   N—N6!
If now 2 R—N1, N—Q5 wins a piece.
    2 PxN   QxR
Black has won the Exchange.

165 1 ....   N—B6ch
    2 K—Q1   ....
Or 2 K—B1 with the same result
    2 ....   P—K7ch!
    3 KxP   N—Q5ch
Followed by 4 . . . NxB and wins.

166 1 ...   RxNch!
    2 PxR   N—K6ch
    3 K moves   NxB
With Bishop, Knight and Pawn for a Rook, Black has a comfortable win.

167 1 ....   BxN
    2 PxB   N—B7
Winning the Exchange, as he threatens . . . NxPch in addition to . . . NxR.

168 1 ....   N—B4
Wins the Exchange, as White cannot play 2 R—Q7.
    2 R/N7—N1 N—Q6 and wins

169 1 ....   P—Q5!
White is lost, for if the attacked Knight moves, 2 . . . N—N6ch wins his Queen.

170 1 ....   RxR
    2 RxR   BxN
    3 KxB   NxBPch
Black wins a Pawn and the Exchange. (Another way is 1 . . . RxNch; 2 RxR, BxR etc.)

171 1 ....   RxPch!
    2 KxR   NxBPch
    3 K moves   NxR
Black has won two Pawns.

172 1 ....   NxBP!!
    2 RxN   ....
If 2 KxN, N—N5ch wins the Queen. If 2 B—B3, N/B7—N5; 3 BxN, NxB and White can resign.
    2 ....   R—B8ch
    3 B—B1   RxR
    4 N/R4—B5   PxN
    5 NxP   QxRch!
    Resigns
For if 6 KxQ, N—N5ch wins.

173 1 ....   N—K5ch!
    2 PxN   R—KB1
Black wins the Queen.

174 1 ....   QxNch!
    2 KxQ   N—K5ch
    3 K moves   NxQ
Black has won a piece.

175 1 ....   B—R6!
If now 2 PxB, N—B6ch wins the Queen; or 2 P—KB4, Q—N3! winning the Queen because of the double threat 3 . . . QxP mate and 3 . . . N—B6ch.
    2 K—R1   BxPch!
    3 KxB   Q—B6ch
    4 K—N1   Q—N5ch
    5 K—R1   N—B6

6 Q—Q1   Q—R6
   Resigns
White must give up his Queen to
stop mate.

176   1 ....   QxNch!
        2 KxQ   NxQPch
        3 K moves   NxQ
Black has won a second Pawn.

177   1 ....   RxB!
   For 2 QxR allows mate, and if
2 RxR, N—B6ch wins.
        2 P—KR3   N—B6ch!
        3 K—B2   RxRch
           Resigns

178   1 ....   QxB!
        2 PxQ   N—K7ch
        3 K moves   NxQ
Black has won a piece.

179   1 ....   N—B7ch
Black wins the Queen.

180   1 ....   QxNch!
        2 QxQ   N—K6ch
        3 K moves   NxQ
Black has won a piece.

181   White's first move threatens
mate, winning the Knight at Queen
Rook 7:
        1 Q—Q4!   Resigns

182   Here too White wins at once
with a double threat:
        1 Q—N5!   Resigns

183   1 NxN   BxN
        2 Q—Q4!   B—R4
        3 P—QN4   KR—Q1
        4 Q—B5 and wins
White wins a piece.

184   1 BxB   RxB
        2 RxR   NxR
        3 Q—N5ch and wins
White wins a piece.

185   1 R—K8ch!   RxR
        2 PxR/Qch   KxQ
        3 R—K3ch! and wins
   If Black interposes, 4 BxPch
wins the Knight. If 3 . . . K—Q1 or
. . . K—B1; 4 BxP wins the Knight
because of the threatened 5 R—K8
mate.

186   1 Q—Q4! and wins
   Black must stop the mate, thereby
losing his Knight.

187   1 Q—B3ch   K moves
        2 Q—K1! and wins
White wins the Rook or Bishop.

188   White's mate threat wins the
Bishop:
        1 Q—K4 and wins

189   1 Q—Q8! and wins
   White threatens QxB as well as
R—B8ch.

190   1 R—B7!!   QxR/B2
        2 RxN!   Resigns
   If 2 . . . QxR; 3 QxNP mate or
2 . . . QxQ; 3 RxR mate.

191   1 Q—K4 and wins
   Protecting himself against the
mate, Black succumbs to QxB.

192   1 Q—B5 and wins
   Black can parry the mating threat
only at the cost of giving up his
Rook.

193   1 NxN   RxN
        2 R—R8ch   K—R2
        3 B—K4ch   Resigns
White wins the Rook.

194   1 P—K5   N—Q4
        2 BxPch   KxB
        3 NxN   BxN
        4 Q—Q3ch   ....
White wins the Bishop.

195   1 BxP!   PxB
        2 Q—N4ch and wins
White forks King and Knight.

196   1 Q—B3!   Resigns
White wins a piece.

197   1 RxP!   RxR
        2 BxRch   KxB
        3 Q—B4ch and wins
White forks King and Bishops.

198   1 N—N5!   N—B3
   If 1 . . . BxN; 2 QxRP mate. If
1 . . . QxB; 2 BxPch, K—R1; 3
NxBP mate.
        2 BxPch   K—R1
        3 NxBP mate

208 · SOLUTIONS ·

199 1 B—R6ch!   K—N1
If 1 . . . KxB; 2 Q—R5ch forces mate. If 1 . . . K—R1; 2 N—B7ch wins the Queen.
    2 NxN   BxN
    3 QxPch and wins
White continues 4 QxQB.

200 1 B—Q4!   R—KN1
If 1 . . . BxB; 2 QxBch wins the Knight. If 1 . . . N—B5; 2 BxBch, KxB; 3 Q—Q4ch forks King and Knight.
    2 BxBch   RxB
    3 Q—Q4   R—QN1
    4 R—N1   Q—N2
    5 B—N3 and wins
White has trapped the Knight.

201 1 N—R7!   RxN
If 1 . . . Q—B2; 2 R—K8ch wins.
    2 P—Q8/Qch   BxQ
    3 QxBch   K—N2
    4 BxN   PxB
    5 Q—Q4ch   . . . .
White wins the Rook.

202 1 P—B6!   PxP
If 1 . . . NxP; 2 Q—N8ch etc.
    2 BxN   RxB
    3 Q—N4ch and wins
White wins a Rook.

203 1 N—Q8ch!   . . . .
Not 1 QxR, QxN; 2 QxB, QxR.
    1 . . . .   QxN
    2 QxRch   K—B1
    3 QxB and wins

204 1 RxB!   RxR
If 1 . . . QxQ; 2 RxRch!
    2 Q—K8ch and wins
White forces mate.

205 1 P—KB4   B—Q3
    2 P—K5   B—B4ch
    3 K—R1   N—N1
    4 Q—Q5 and wins
This "triple attack" wins because of the mate threat.

206 1 P—KB4   B—Q3
    2 Q—K8ch   . . . .
White wins the Rook.

207 1 RxNch   PxR
    2 QxPch   . . . .
White wins the Rook.

208 1 RxBch   KxR
    2 Q—Q4ch   . . . .
White wins the Rook.

209 1 BxB   RxB
    2 Q—Q3   . . . .
White wins a piece.

210 1 RxB   NxR
    2 Q—R4ch and wins
After 3 QxN White has two pieces for a Rook.

211 1 RxB   RxR
    2 Q—B6   . . . .
White wins a Rook.

212 1 P—KR3!   N—R3
    2 Q—K4   . . . .
Wins the Rook; Black must guard against QxP mate.

213 1 R—N5ch!   N—N3
    2 Q—K6ch   . . . .
White wins the Bishop.

214 1 BxN   QxB
    2 Q—Q5ch   . . . .
White wins the Knight.

215 1 N—N5!   PxN
If 1 . . . R—KB3; 2 QxB, QxQ; 3 NxQ wins a piece.
    2 QxNPch and wins
After 3 QxRch White is the Exchange ahead.

216 1 NxQP!   PxN
    2 RxN!   QxR
    3 Q—K8!   . . . .
Threatens 4 Q—KR8 mate.
    3 . . . .   R—B1
    4 NxRch   QxN
Else White mates.
    5 QxQ   Resigns

217 1 NxP!   NxN
    2 Q—R5ch   N—N3
    3 Q—Q5 and wins
White's mate threat enables him to win the Rook.

218 1 BxB   KxB
Or 1 . . . R—K1; 2 B—K5, P—B3; 3 Q—K4! remaining a piece ahead.
    2 Q—K5ch   N—B3
    3 R—Q6!   . . . .
White wins the Knight.

219   1 Q—B7!   R/N1—Q1
2 BxN and wins
Black cannot recapture.

220   1 NxN   BxN
2 BxB   RxB
3 Q—Q5ch   ....
White wins the Queen Rook.

221   1 BxN   PxB
No better is 1 . . . QxB.
2 Q—R3ch   ...
White wins the Bishop.

222   1 P—Q5   N—K2
2 Q—R4ch and wins

223   1 N—R6ch!   PxN
2 Q—N4ch and wins
White's next is 3 QxR.

224   1 R—R3!   P—R3
White threatened 2 RxPch!, KxR;
3 Q—R5 mate. If 1 . . . P—KN3;
2 PxP!, RxP; 3 RxPch!, KxR; 4
Q—R5ch, R—R3; 5 Q—B7ch followed by mate.
2 Q—Q2! and wins
White threatens 3 QxB as well as
3 QxPch! (or 3 RxPch!), PxQ; 4
RxP mate.

225   1 NxB   RxN
2 P—B4 and wins

226   1 BxPch!   RxB
If 1 . . . KxB; 2 Q—N3ch wins
the Bishop.
2 PxP   N—N5
Black dare not play . . . NxP??
losing his Queen.
3 P—K6   ....
The double attack wins back a
piece.

227   1 P—K3   N—B4
Or 1 . . . N—N4; 2 Q—R4.
2 Q—N4 and wins

228   1 P—B6   RxP
If 1 . . R—N1; 2 Q—Q6ch wins.
2 Q—Q8ch   Resigns
White wins the Rook.

229   1 Q—K7ch   KxN
2 P—KN4ch   Resigns

230   1 RxN   PxRch
2 KxP   Resigns
White threatens KxR and also
P—B6ch.

231   1 P—B6ch   KPxP
2 P—K7   Resigns

232   1 BxN   KxB
2 P—B5   PxP
3 PxP   Q—QB3
4 P—B6ch and wins

233   1 P—B3   Q—R5
2 QxQ   PxQ
3 P—K4 and wins

234   1 BxPch!   NxB
2 R—Q7ch   K—B1
3 NxNch   K—N1
4 N—B8 dis ch   ....
White mates next move.

235   1 P—Q7   R—Q1
2 Q—R5 and wins
White wins a piece.

236   1 RxB!   KxR
If 1 . . . QxR; 2 B—B6 wins the
Queen.
2 B—B6ch!   QxB
3 N—R5ch   Resigns
White wins the Queen.

237   1 N—K8!   Q—K2
2 Q—KN3   QxN
White threatened mate.
3 QxR and wins

238   1 NxN   QxN
2 BxPch   Resigns
White wins the Queen.

239   1 QxPch!!   KxQ
Or 1 . . . RxQ; 2 RxQch and 3
RxB.
2 RxRch   QxR
3 N—B5ch and wins
White is a piece up after 4 NxR.

240   1 P—N5!   PxP
Forced.
2 RxN!   RxR
3 RxR   QxR
4 Q—B8ch and wins
White wins the Rook.

241   1 RxB!   RxR
2 Q—Q4   Q—K4
3 R—K1!   Resigns
If 3 . . . QxQ; 4 RxR mate. If 3
. . . QxR; 4 Q—N7 mate.

242   1 R—B5   ....
White wins a piece.

243   1 B—B7!!   KxB

If 1 . . . QxB; 2 RxR winning
the Exchange as Black's Bishop is
pinned. If 1 . . . RxR; 2 QxNPch,
K—B1; 3 Q—N8ch, K—K2; 4 Q—
K8ch, K—Q3; 5 Q—K6 mate.

　　　2 RxR   QxR
　　　3 Q—N7ch   . . . .
White wins the Rook.

244   1 Q—KR8ch   K—N4
　　　2 Q—K5ch and wins

(2 Q—Q8ch also wins the Bishop.)

245   1 NxP!   PxN
　　　2 Q—N5ch   . . . .
White wins back the sacrificed
material and remains a Pawn ahead.

246   1 P—Q5!   BxP
　　　2 NxBP   . . . .
White wins the Exchange.

247   1 RxB!   RxR
　　　2 RxR   QxR
　　　3 Q—KN4ch   . . . .
White wins the Rook.

248   1 N—R4!   BxN
　　　2 P—Q6!   . . . .
This secondary threat explains the
previous move.

　　　2 . . . .   PxP
　　　3 BxB   N—B3
　　　4 BxR   RxB
　　　5 PxB   . . . .
White has won the Exchange.

249   1 RxB!   RxR
　　　2 Q—K5   . . . .
The threat of 3 QxNP mate wins
the Rook.

250   1 Q—Q4   P—B3
　　　2 NxB   RxN
　　　3 QxR   QxB
　　　4 R—K1   . . . .
White has won the Exchange.

251   1 B—R6   NxQ
　　　2 BxPch   K—N1
　　　3 BxN dis ch   B—N4
　　　4 RxB mate

252   1 NxP!   PxN
　　　2 BxN   PxB
　　　3 RxB!   RxR
　　　4 Q—N3ch   . . . .

This is the point. White continues
5 QxR with a Pawn ahead.

253   1 . . . .   P—Q6!
　　　2 RxP   RxR
　　　3 QxR   P—K5
　　　4 BxN   PxB
Black wins a piece.

254   1 . . . .   B—B3
Black wins a piece.

255   1 . . . .   QxQ
　　　2 RxQ   B—N5
　　　3 R—Q1   R—B7
Black wins a piece.

256   1 . . . .   P—KN4
　　　2 B—K3   P—N5
Black wins a piece.

257   1 . . . .   RxN!
　　　2 RxR   NxP!
　　　Resigns
For if 3 BxN, QxRch and Black
mates next move.

258   1 . . . .   Q—K3!
　　　2 Q—B2   RxPch!
　　　3 KxR   Q—R3 mate

259   1 . . . .   Q—B3 and wins

260   1 . . . .   R—KN6ch and wins

261   1 . . . .   R—K1!
　　　2 Q—KB4   Q—Q5!
Black wins a piece.

262   1 . . . .   KNxKP!
　　　2 NxN   Q—R5ch and wins
After 3 . . . QxB or 3 . . . BxB,
depending on White's reply, Black
is a Pawn ahead.

263   1 . . . .   RxPch!!
　　　2 QxR   B—N3ch
　　　3 Q—K4   . . . .
If 3 K—B3 or 3 K—B4, R—B7
mate.
　　　3 . . . .   BxQch
Black is the Exchange ahead.

264   1 . . . .   BxB
　　　2 KxB   Q—KN8
Black wins a piece.

265   1 . . . .   NxBP!
　　　2 KxN   NxN
　　　3 BxN   Q—R5ch
Black continues 4 . . . QxB.

266
1	RxQP!
2 RxR	Q—R6ch
3 K—N1	QxRPch
4 K—B1	Q—R8ch

Followed by 5 . . . QxR/Q5 and wins.

267
1	BxN
2 PxB	RxB!
3 PxR	QxPch

Black wins the Rook.

268
1	QxRch!
2 NxQ	RxQ
3 PxR	R—Q8ch

Black wins the Knight.

269
| 1 .... | P—B3 |
| 2 B—B4 | Q—R4ch |

Black wins the Knight.

270
| 1 .... | Q—B2ch! |
| 2 P—N3 | Q—K2! |

Black wins the Rook because of the simultaneous threat of . . . Q—K7 mate.

271
1	BxPch!
2 KxB	NxP
3 Q—K2	NxB
4 QxN	BxN
5 QxB	Q—R5ch

Black wins the Rook.

272
| 1 .... | Q—K8ch |
| 2 R—Q1 | Q—K5! |

Threatens mate.
| 3 R—Q3 | Q—R8ch! |
| 4 R—Q1 | QxP and wins |

Black still threatens mate and thus gains time to pick up the remaining White Pawn.

273
1	BxN
2 PxB	NxKP!
3 PxN	QxPch and wins

Black continues 4 . . . QxB/Q6.

274
| 1 .... | BxPch! |
| 2 KxB | Q—N5ch |

If now 3 K—R1, Q—B6 mate.
| 3 K—B1 | QxRch |

If now 4 R—K1, Q—B6ch forcing checkmate.
4 K—N2	Q—N5ch
5 K—B1	Q—B6ch
6 K—K1	QxRch

Black wins the Bishop too.

275
| 1 .... | RxBch! |
| 2 PxR | QxKPch |

Black wins the Rook.

276 If Black tries to win a piece by the double attack 1 . . . Q—K4? he fails after 2 N—B3! The right way is:
| 1 .... | RxN! |
| 2 RxR | Q—K4! |

Black wins the Rook because of the threat . . . Q—R7 mate.

277
| 1 .... | RxN! |
| 2 PxR | B—Q5ch |

Black wins the Rook.

278
| 1 .... | NxQP! |
| 2 PxN | Q—R5ch |

Black continues 3 . . . QxB.

279
| 1 .... | R—Q4! |
| 2 B—B4 | .... |

After 2 B—K8 Black has the same winning move.
| 2 .... | P—QN4 and wins |

280
| 1 .... | P—K6! |

Threatens . . . P—K7.
| 2 R—K1 | PxP |

Black wins a piece.

281
1	P—N3!
2 Q—R4	BxKBPch!
3 KxB	P—N4ch

Black wins the Queen and comes out a Rook ahead.

282
| 1 .... | P—KN4! |
| 2 B—N3 | P—N5 |

If the attacked Knight moves, 3 . . . N—K5 wins a piece.
| 3 P—QR3 | PxN! |
| 4 PxB | PxP |

The double attack wins a piece.

283
| 1 .... | P—Q5! |

Threatens 2 . . . QxQch! 3 KxQ, P—Q6ch winning a piece.
| 2 QxQ | PxQ |

Black wins a piece, for if 3 N moves, P—Q7ch wins the Rook.

284
1	NxPch!
2 PxN	Q—Q5ch
3 K—R1	RxR and wins

285
| 1 .... | RxB |
| 2 RxR | BxPch |

Black continues 3 . . . BxR.

212 · SOLUTIONS ·

286 1 .... Q—B5!
This wins a piece, as White cannot guard both Rook and Knight.

287 1 .... Q—N3!!
Threatening . . . QxP mate and also attacking White's Bishop. White can stop the mate only by losing his Bishop. Instead this follows:
2 BxQ N—K7 mate!

288 1 .... NxBch
Forcing White's reply.
2 QxN Q—Q5ch and wins
Black continues 3 . . . QxN/B6.

289 1 .... RxBP!
If now 2 RxR, RxPch; 3 PxR, BxRch; 4 QxB, QxQch and 5 . . . QxR. If 2 PxR, RxPch and mate next move.
2 B—R2 RxP!
3 PxR/R3 RxR mate

290 1 .... Q—R6!!
Threatening not only . . . QxB but also . . . N—N6ch and mate next move.
2 PxQ N—B7 dbl ch
3 K—N1 NxP mate

291 1 .... R—Q6
2 QR—B1 ....
White can stop mate only by losing his Bishop.
2 .... R—R6 mate

292 1 .... PxP!
2 R—Q2 PxP dis ch
If now 3 K—N2, R—KR6! saves everything for Black.
3 KxP B—B2!!
Black wins, for if 4 BxR, BxPch and 5 . . . BxR.

293 1 .... Q—K2!
Attacking the Rook and also threatening . . . Q—K8 mate.
2 P—KR4 Q—K8ch
3 K—R2 QxPch
Black continues 4 . . . QxR.

294 1 .... P—B4
2 N—B3 P—B5 and wins

295 White's discovered attack wins the Queen because of the threat 2 Q—R8 mate:
1 N—Q5! Resigns

296 White's discovered attack wins the Queen or forces checkmate:
1 N—K6! QxB
2 N—Q5! Q—K5
3 N/Q5—B7 mate

297 1 RxPch! ....
If now 1 . . . PxR; 2 B—N6ch wins the Queen. Or 1 . . . BxR; 2 B—N5ch with the same result. So Black must move his King, remaining with a decidedly inferior game.

298 1 B—K7! R—K1
2 B—N4 Resigns
By threatening mate, White wins the Queen.

299 1 QxR QxQ
2 P—B8/Q dis ch Resigns

300 1 B—R6! R—N1?
This loses a whole Rook instead of "only" the Exchange.
2 B—B4ch ....
White wins a whole Rook.

301 1 NxN! QxQ
Or 1 . . . QxN; 2 Q—N7 mate.
2 NxNch K—R1
3 N—B7 mate

302 1 NxB! Resigns
If 1 . . . RxN; 2 QxR; or 1 . . . RxQ; 2 NxQch and White wins a Rook in either event.

303 1 N—N5! QxN
2 BxB and wins

304 1 RxN! NxR
2 RxN ....
If now 2 . . . QxR; 3 N—R6ch wins the Queen.

305 1 P—Q6! BxB
2 PxB R—K1
3 KxP PxN
4 PxP RxP
5 P—N6!
White will win the Queen Rook Pawn and Queen Pawn, but aside from that, his far advanced passed Pawn assures him an easy win.

306 1 Q—N4 P—N3
2 N—R6ch Resigns

307 1 P—KB3 B—R4
2 P—KB4! ....

If 2 . . . BxB; 3 PxN or 2 . . . PxP; 3 BxB. White wins a piece in either event.

308 1 N—K6!   Q—R4ch
If 1 . . . QxB; 2 N/N5—B7 mate.
    2 B—Q2   QxBch
    3 QxQ   NxQ
    4 N/N5—B7 mate

309 1 B—B4!   RxRch
If 1 . . . QxB; 2 RxRch etc.
    2 BxR!   Q—R4
    3 R—K1!   Resigns
If the Bishop moves, 4 Q—K8ch! decides.

310 1 NxBP!   QxN
Else his Rook goes lost.
    2 BxPch   Resigns
White wins the Queen.

311 1 PxP   BxP
Or 1 . . . NxQBP; 2 BxN winning a piece.
    2 BxB   NxB
    3 RxN!   Resigns
If 3 . . . QxR/B4; 4 RxRch etc.

312 1 N—K6ch!   QxN
    2 Q—R5ch   K—N1
If 2 . . . K—B3; 3 P—N5 mate. Or 2 . . . P—N3; 3 Q—R7ch, K—B3; 4 QxP mate.
    3 B—R7ch   K—R1
    4 B—N6 dis ch   K—N1
    5 Q—R7 mate

313 1 N—N5!   R—Q1
If 1 . . . QxQ; 2 NxP/B7 mate!
    2 QxQ   RxQ
    3 NxP/B7ch   K—N1
    4 P—R5   Resigns
The Rook is trapped, leaving Black with a lost ending.

314 1 B—Q5!   Resigns
If 1 . . . RxR; 2 Q—N8 mate. If 1 . . . RxB; 2 RxR mate or 1 . . . QxB; 2 RxRch followed by mate.

315 1 N—N5!   BxN
    2 BxB   NxPch
    3 RxN   ....
White continues 4 BxR.

316 1 Q—K6ch!   K—R2
No better is 1 . . . K—R4
    2 N—B6ch   PxN
    3 QxQ   Resigns

317 1 BxPch!   KxB
    2 QxQ   Resigns

318 1 N—Q5!   NxN
If 1 . . . QxQ; 2 NxNch wins a piece.
    2 QxQ   NxQ
    3 BxB!   QN—Q2
    4 BxR   KxB
    5 P—K5   N—Q4
    6 BxN   PxB
    7 P—K6 and wins

319 1 BxN!   PxB
    2 NxP/B6ch!   BxN
    3 RxNch!   Resigns
White continues 4 QxQ.

320 1 RxP!   QxKB
    2 B—B5!   QxQ
Expecting 3 RxQ??, R—Q8ch and Black forces mate.
    3 RxBch!   QxR
    4 RxQ mate

321 1 N—B6!!   Resigns
No matter how Black plays he is checkmated. For example: 1 . . . NxQ; 2 RxP mate. Or 1 . . . PxN; 2 QxRP mate. Or 1 . . . P—R3; 2 Q—R7 mate.

322 1 P—Q5!   Resigns
In saving his Queen, Black loses his Knight.

323 1 NxP!   BxQ
"Best" is 1 . . . PxN; 2 QxB and White wins easily.
    2 BxPch   K—K2
    3 N—Q5 mate

324 1 N—Q5!   Q—R5
    2 B—N5ch!   QxB
    3 NxPch   Resigns
Black loses his Queen.

325 1 RxN!   QxR
    2 NxP   Q—B1
    3 BxB   QxB
    4 N—N6!   B—B3
    5 N—K7ch!   K—R1
    6 QxB!   PxQ
    7 BxP mate

326 1 P—B7 dis ch   K—R2
On 1 . . . B—N2 White makes a new Queen.
    2 Q—B5ch   K—R1
    3 Q—B6ch   K—R2

4 P—N6ch Resigns
Black loses his Queen.

327 1 N—N6! R—R2
2 N/B3xB QxN
3 NxB RxN
4 BxPch Resigns
White wins a whole Rook.

328 1 QxN!! QxQ
2 P—QB4 Q—Q2
3 RxPch K—R1
4 R—N8 dbl ch KxR
5 R—N1ch Q—N5
6 RxQ mate

329 1 N—Q6 R—K2
If 1 . . . R—B1 White wins the
Exchange in the same way. But if
1 . . . R—KN1?; 2 N—B7 mate!
2 NxB . . . .
White wins the Exchange by 3
BxR etc.

330 1 RxB! QxR
2 N—KN6! Resigns
If 2 . . . QxQ; 3 N/Q5—K7 mate.

331 1 . . . . BxN!
2 QxR N—K4
Threatens . . . Q—N5.
3 K—R1 BxNPch!
4 KxB Q—N5ch
5 K—R1 Q—K5ch
6 K—N1 N—B6ch
7 K—N2 N—R5 dbl ch
8 K—N3 Q—N7ch
9 KxN B—K2ch
And Black mates next move.

332 1 . . . . N—Q6!
2 R—Q1 Q—R8ch
3 K—K2 N—B5ch!
Resigns
If 4 PxN, QxRch; 5 K—K3, Q—
Q6 mate. If 4 K—B3, QxNPch wins
the Queen.

333 1 . . . . B—K6!
Resigns
Black threatens mate as well as
. . . BxBch.

334 1 . . . . RxKP!
2 QxR Q—B6ch
3 Q—B2 QxQ mate

335 1 . . . . N—B2
Resigns
White must lose the Knight or the
Bishop.

336 1 . . . . NxP!
2 QxQ NxRch
3 K—B1 BxQ
4 KxN RxN
Resigns

337 1 . . . . NxN
2 QxN N—N5ch!
Resigns
White loses his Queen.

338 1 . . . . NxP!
If now 2 BxB, N—Q6ch followed
by . . . QxB. If 2 PxN, BxB etc.

339 1 . . . . QxR!
2 RxQ RxN
3 RxR RxR
4 Q—R3 . . . .
After 4 Q—R1 Black wins the
Queen the same way.
4 . . . . RxPch
5 K—R1 RxP dis ch
Resigns
White loses his Queen.

340 1 . . . . N—K6
Forcing White's reply.
2 R—K1 N—B5ch!
3 BxN RxR and wins

341 1 . . . . BxQP!
2 QxB BxPch!
3 NxB RxQ
Resigns

342 1 . . . . NxBP!
2 KxN BxNPch
Resigns
White loses his Queen.

343 1 . . . . Q—B8ch
2 K—R2 Q—B5ch
If now 3 K—N1, N—B6ch wins
White's Queen.
3 K—R1 Q—KB8ch
4 K—R2 QxR and wins

344 1 . . . . P—Q6!
If now 2 QxP, QxB etc.
2 BxQ PxQ and wins
White loses his Rook or Bishop.

345 1 . . . . B—KR6!
2 QxR B—QB4ch
If now 3 R/K4—Q4, BxRch; 5
RxB, Q—K8 mate.
3 K—R1 BxPch!
4 KxB Q—N5ch

If now 5 K—R1, Q—B6 mate.
5 K—B1 Q—B6ch
6 K—K1 Q—B7 mate

346 1 .... N—KB6ch!
If now 2 K—R1, NxR wins.
2 PxN Q—N3ch
3 K—R1 N—N6ch!
4 RPxN QxQ
Resigns

347 1 .... RxBch!
2 KxR B—Q6ch!
Resigns
White loses his Queen.

348 1 .... N—KN6!
2 QxQ N/Q5—K7 mate

349 1 QxRch! KxQ
2 B—B2 dis ch! and wins
White continues 3 BxQ.

350 1 B—R7ch K—R1
2 B—N8 dis ch! KxB
Or 2 ... B—R3; 3 Q—R7 mate.
3 Q—R7 mate

351 1 N—B7!! Q—B3
If 1 ... KxN; 2 PxP dis ch wins
Black's Queen.
2 PxP and wins
Black cannot save his Queen,
Rook, and Bishop.

352 1 NxP! RxQ
If 1 ... NxB; 2 N—N5 dis ch,
K—R3; 3 RxP mate.
2 NxR dis ch K—B3
3 NxQ and wins
White comes out the Exchange
ahead.

353 1 RxN! PxR
2 QxRch! KxQ
3 PxP dis ch and wins
White continues 4 PxQ.

354 1 QxNch! K—K2
If 1 ... KxN; 2 N—B6 dis ch
and mate.
2 N—Q6 Resigns

355 1 R—Q7ch R—B2
2 RxRch KxR
3 B—B8 dis ch ....
White continues 4 BxB.

356 1 R—KR1 ....
Threatens 2 K—N2 dis ch and
mate.

1 .... K—R4
2 K—N3 dis ch ....
White wins the Bishop.

357 1 Q—Q5 ....
Threatening a discovered check—
such as R—B6 dis ch.
1 .... Q—B8ch
If 1 ... K—R1; 2 Q—Q8ch and
mate next move.
2 R—B1 dis ch Resigns

358 1 Q—B5ch R—K2
2 N—N6ch! KxB
If 2 ... PxN; 3 R—R8ch, KxB;
4 PxN dis ch, K—K3; 5 R—K1ch
and White mates soon.
3 PxN dis ch K—N1
If 3 ... KxN; 4 Q—B5 mate.
4 NxRch K—R1
5 N—N6ch K—N1
6 Q—B8ch! RxQ
7 RxR mate

359 1 P—Q5 dis ch Resigns

360 1 B—R5ch! P—N3
2 NxNP! N—N3
If 2 ... PxN; 3 BxP mate.
3 N—K5 mate

361 1 BxN NxB
2 BxP dis ch K—Q2
3 BxB Resigns
If 3 ... RxB; 4 N—K5ch wins
the Bishop.

362 1 NxPch! BxN
2 RxB BxB
3 RxPch K—R1
4 RxP dis ch K—N1
5 R—KN7ch K—R1
6 R—QB7disch K—N1
7 RxB Resigns

363 1 RxB! QxR
2 BxPch K—N1
3 P—B5 dis ch ....
White continues 4 PxQ.

364 1 QxPch! KxQ
2 PxP dis ch K—N3
3 PxP ....
White plays 4 PxR/Q, leaving
him a whole Rook ahead.

365 1 R—R8ch! KxR
2 P—K6 dis ch Q—N2
3 BxQch Resigns
Black has only two pieces for
the Queen.

366 White wins the Queen:
    1 N—B5 dis ch Resigns

367 1 Q—R5ch! K—N2
    If 1 . . . KxQ; 2 N—B7 dis ch,
B—N4; 3 RxB mate.
    2 Q—R7ch K—B1
    3 QxR N—K2
    4 RxBch QxR
    5 N—R7ch Resigns
White wins the Queen.

368 1 N—R5 PxN
    2 BxPch K—R1
    3 B—N6 dis ch K—N1
    4 Q—R7ch K—B1
    5 B—R6ch K—K2
    6 QxPch K—Q1
    7 QxR mate

369 1 R—N3ch! PxR
    2 BxPch! KxB
    3 RPxP dis ch K—N1
    4 R—R8 mate

370 1 R—K7! BxN
    2 RxPch K—R1
    3 RxB dis ch K—N1
    4 RxB Resigns

371 1 RxNch KxR
    2 NxP dis ch and wins

372 1 Q—R8ch N—N1
    2 QxPch! KxQ
    3 BxB dis ch K—R1
    4 RxNch! KxR
    5 R—N1ch K—R1
    6 B—B6 mate

373 1 R—K7! K—N1
    If 1 . . . QxR; 2 P—B6 dis ch
wins the Queen.
    2 RxRP and wins

374 1 QxRPch! BxQ
    2 P—B7 dis ch P—K4
    3 BxP mate

375 1 N—N6ch! PxN
    2 PxNP dis ch and wins

376 1 QxPch! QxQ
    2 RxQch KxR
    3 R—R1ch B—R7
    4 RxBch K—N2
    5 B—R6ch K—R2
    6 BxR mate

377 1 R—N7ch K—B1
    2 RxQP dis ch K—N1
    3 R—KN7ch K—B1
    4 R—N7 dis ch K—N1
    5 RxRch N—B1
    6 RxN mate

378 1 QxPch! KxQ
    2 R—QR3ch K—N2
    3 B—R6ch K—R1
    4 B—B8 mate

379 1 QxPch! KxQ
    2 B—R5ch! KxR
    3 B—B7 mate

380 1 B—B8 dis ch B—R4
    2 QxBch! PxQ
    3 R—R6 mate

381 1 NxNP! KxN
    2 QxPch! KxQ
    3 BxN mate

382 1 P—N4! N—B5
    If 1 . . . N—B3; 2 B—Q5 dis ch
wins the Knight.
    2 BxN dis ch and wins

383 1 N—K6 dis ch! PxQ
    2 B—N7 mate

384 1 QxRP! PxQ
    2 PxP dis ch K—B1
    3 R—N8ch! KxR
    4 P—R7ch K—B1
    5 P—R8/Q mate

385 1 . . . . BxN!
    2 RxR P—K7 dis ch
    3 K—R1 P—K8/Q mate

386 1 . . . . QxB!
    So that if 2 QxQ, R—K8ch, 3
B—B1, RxBch!; 4 RxR, P—B7
mate.
    2 Q—B1 Q—N7!
    3 Q—B1 QxR!
    4 QxQ R—K8ch!
    5 QxR P—B7 dis ch
Black mates in two moves.

387 1 . . . . N—Q5 dis ch!
    2 N—Q2 RxNch
    3 RxR N—B6ch
Followed by 4 . . . NxR.

388 1 . . . . N—R5 dis ch
    If now 2 K—N1, Q—KN5 mate.
    2 K—K1 NxN mate

389	1	NxP!
	2 QxN	QxQch
	3 KxQ	P—B6 dis ch
	4 NxB	PxR! and wins

390	1	N—N6ch!
	2 PxN	PxP dis ch
	3 BxR	Q—R5 mate

391	1	RxNPch!
	2 KxR	RxPch!
	3 BxR	P—K6 dis ch
	Resigns	

If 4 R—Q5 (forced), QxBch; 5 K—R1, QxRch; 6 K—N2, Q—B7ch; 7 K—R1, P—K7 and wins.

| 392 | 1 .... | QxRch! |
| | 2 KxQ | N—B4 dis ch |

Followed by 3 ... NxQ.

| 393 | 1 .... | QxB! |
| | 2 PxQ | R—Q1 dis ch |

Followed by 3 ... RxQ.

394	1	QxN!
	2 BxQ	P—K6 dis ch
	3 Q—N2	....

If 3 Q—B3, BxQch; 4 RxB, NxP; 5 R—Q1, NxB; 6 RxN, B—B4 with a winning endgame.

	3	BxQch
	4 KxB	NxP
	5 R—R4	....

If 5 R—Q1, RxN!; 6 BxR, P—K7 and wins.

	5	KR—Q1
	6 B—N6	R—Q7ch
	7 K—B3	RxN!
	8 PxR	P—K7 and wins

| 395 | 1 .... | P—K7 dis ch |

Black wins, for if 2 R—B2, QxRch etc.

396	1	RxKNP!
	2 PxQ	RxRch
	3 BxR	R—Q7 dis ch
	4 K—N1	B—Q5ch
	5 B—B2	RxRch
	6 Q—K1	RxQ mate

| 397 | 1 QxPch! | KxQ |
| | 2 BxP dbl ch | K—N3 |

If 2 ... K—K2; 3 R—B7 mate.

	3 B—B7ch	KxP
	4 B—B1ch	K—N5
	5 R—B4ch	K—N4
	6 P—R4ch	K—R3
	7 R—B6 mate	

398	1 Q—R5ch!	NxQ
	2 PxP dbl ch	K—N3
	3 B—B2ch	K—N4
	4 R—B5ch	K—N3

If 4 ... K—N5; 5 P—R3ch leads to quick mate. Likewise if 4 ... K—R5; 5 R—K4ch etc.

	5 R—B6 dbl ch	K—N4
	6 R—N6ch	K—R5
	7 R—K4ch	N—B5
	8 RxNch	K—R4
	9 P—N3!	....

Followed by 10 R—R4 mate.

399	1 Q—Q8ch!	KxQ
	2 B—R5 dbl ch	K—K1
	3 R—Q8 mate	

400	1 NxBP!	PxN
	2 N—B6ch!	QxN
	3 Q—Q8ch!	BxQ
	4 B—N5 mate	

401	1 Q—Q7ch!	BxQ
	2 N—Q6 dbl ch	K—Q1
	3 N—B7ch	K—B1
	4 R—K8ch!	BxR
	5 R—Q8 mate	

402	1 N—K7 dbl ch	K—R1
	2 N—N6ch!	PxN
	3 RPxN dis ch	Q—R5
	4 RxQ mate	

| 403 | 1 NxP! | N—K2 |

If 1 ... either NxN; 2 RxNch is deadly.

	2 NxN!	QxQ
	3 N—B6 dbl ch	K—B1
	4 BxN mate	

| 404 | 1 BxP! | BxR |
| | 2 BxP dbl ch! Resigns | |

If 2 ... KxB; 3 Q—K6 mate. Or 2 ... K—Q1; 3 Q—K8ch winning Black's Queen.

405	1 Q—Q8ch!	KxQ
	2 B—KN5dblch	K—K1
	3 R—Q8 mate	

| 406 | 1 Q—Q8ch! | KxQ |
| | 2 B—KN5dblch | K—K1 |

Or 2 ... K—B2; 3 B—Q8 mate.

| | 3 R—Q8 mate | |

| 407 | 1 RxNP! | PxR |
| | 2 Q—R7ch | N—Q2 |

If 2 . . . K—Q1; 3 Q—R8ch is decisive.

      3 BxN!   Q—N1

If 3 . . . QxB; 4 QxQch, KxQ; 5 RxR and White wins easily.

      4 R—N7ch!   KxR

If 4 . . . RxR; 5 QxQ and wins. Or 4 . . . K—Q1; 5 QxQch and wins.

      5 B—B8 dbl ch! and wins

The most beautiful double check ever played. After 5 . . . KxB; 6 QxQch White wins a Rook.

408 1 R—Q7!   QxR
      2 RxNPch!   KxR
      3 B—R6ch   K—R1
      4 N—N6ch!   PxN
      5 PxP   Q—B8ch
      6 K—R4   Q—B6
      7 B—N7 dbl ch   KxB
      8 Q—R7 mate

409 1 Q—Q8ch!   KxQ
      2 B—KN5dblch K—K1
      3 R—Q8 mate

410 1 R—N8 dbl ch! KxR
      2 R—KN1 mate

411 1 N/Q2xN!   NxNch
      2 QxN!   QxQ
      3 N—B6 dbl ch K—Q1
      4 R—K8 mate

412 1 B—Q6 dbl ch! KxB
      2 R—Q3   . . . .
White wins the Queen.

413 1 R—N8ch!   KxR
Or 1 . . . RxR; 2 NxQ etc.
      2 NxQ dbl ch Resigns
White wins the Black Queen without losing his own.

414 1 Q—Q7ch!   BxQ
      2 N—Q6 dbl ch K—Q1
      3 N—B7ch   K—B1
      4 R—K8ch!   BxR
      5 R—Q8 mate

415 1 . . . .   B—Q6 dbl ch
      2 K—K1   R—B8 mate

416 1 . . . .   R—B8 dbl ch!
      2 KxR   Q—B5ch
      3 K—Q2   Q—Q6ch
      4 K—K1   Q—K6ch
      5 K—B1   R—KB1
      Resigns

White is helpless; for example 6 Q—B3, B—R6ch etc.

417 1 . . . .   N—B6 mate!

418 1 . . . .   Q—N7ch!
      2 KxQ   RxNP mate

419 1 . . . .   QxR!
      2 PxQ   B—N5 dbl ch
      3 K—Q1   R—K8 mate

420 1 . . . .   RxBP!
      2 QxQ   RxN mate

421 1 Q—Q5ch!   Resigns
If 1 . . . RxQ; 2 RxR mate.
(If White plays 1 QxQ in the diagram position, Black can make a fight of it with 1 . . . N—B7 dbl ch or . . . N—B5 dis ch.)

422 1 N—Q5   Q—Q1
      2 BxP   Q—Q2
      3 Q—N4!   R—K3
If 3 . . . QxQ; 4 RxR mate.
      4 RxR   QxR
If 4 . . . PxR; 5 N—B6ch.
      5 N—B6ch   K—B1
If 5 . . . QxN; 6 QxBch and mate follows.
      6 B—Q6ch!   QxB
      7 QxBch   K—K2
      8 N—N8 mate

423 1 Q—B4!   Resigns
White threatens 2 Q—N8 mate, and if 1 . . . RxQ; 2 RxN mate.

424 1 R—Q7!   QxR
If 1 . . . NxR; 2 Q—KN4ch, K—R3; 3 R—B5 wins.
      2 QxNch   K—N3
      3 R—B5   Resigns
Black's King cannot escape.

425 1 RxPch!.   QxR
If 1 . . . KxR; 2 BxN, QxB; 3 R—KN1ch forcing mate.
      2 BxNch   R—B2
      3 R—KN1!   QxR
      4 QxRch   K—R1
      5 Q—R5ch   K—N2
      6 Q—R6 mate

426 1 R—B8ch!   QxR
      2 QxPch!   RxQ
      3 RxR mate

427 1 R—Q5ch!   NxR
If 1 . . . K—R3; 2 B—B8ch
wins.
    2 B—K2ch   K—R4
    3 R—QR7ch   R—R3
    4 RxR mate

428 1 R—K5   Q—Q2
    2 RxRch   QxR
    3 P—Q7!   QxP
    4 Q—N8ch   K—R2
    5 Q—R8ch!   NxQ
    6 R—N7 mate

429 1 B—R3!   QxB
    2 Q—K6!   N—Q1
    3 Q—B7ch!   NxQ
    4 N—K6 mate

430 1 Q—R6!   Resigns
If 1 . . . BxQ; 2 N—K7 mate.

431 1 B—B6!   PxB
Or 1 . . . R—KN1; 2 QxNPch!,
RxQ; 3 R—Q8ch and mate follows.
    2 KPxP   R—KN1
    3 R—Q8!   QRxR
    4 RxR   Resigns
White threatens mate, and if 4
. . . RxR; 5 Q—N7 mate.

432 1 Q—K7!   Q—B2
If 1 . . . RxQ; 2 R—B8 mate.
If 1 . . . RxR; 2 Q—N7 mate.
    2 Q—B8ch!   RxQ
    3 RxR mate

433 1 RxP!   Resigns
If 1 . . . RxR; 2 Q—Q8 mate;
if 1 . . . QxR; 2 Q—Q7 mate.

434 1 RxB!   Resigns
If 1 . . . R/N1xR; 2 RxR. Or 1
. . . R/R1xR; 2 RxR. In either case
White has won a piece.

435 1 BxP!   PxB
    2 NxP   R—KN1
    3 R—K8!   Resigns
If 3 . . . RxR; 4 Q—N7 mate. If
3 . . . QxR; 4 Q—B6ch and mate
next move.

436 1 RxB!   QxR
    2 Q—N6   Resigns
There is no defense to the coming
3 QxRP mate.

437 1 R—QB5ch!   K—N1
If 1 . . . N—B2?; 2 QxQ. If 1
. . . R—B2; 2 RxRch, KxR; 3
RxPch with an easy win.
    2 BxP!   RxB
If 2 . . . QxQch; 3 B—N2 dis ch!
and wins.
    3 RxRch   KxR
    4 Q—N2ch   K—N1
    5 R—N5ch   K—B2
    6 Q—N7ch   K—Q3
    7 R—Q5 mate

438 1 R—K8!   QxR
Or 1 . . . RxR; 2 Q—N7 mate.
    2 Q—B6ch   R—N2
    3 QxR mate

439 1 PxP!   NxQ
    2 PxN dis ch   K—N1
    3 R—R8ch!   KxR
    4 P—B7!   B—K2
If 4 . . . Q—R5; 5 PxN/Qch and
mate next move.
    5 R—R1ch   B—R5
    6 P—B8/Q mate

440 1 R—KR3!   QxR
    2 QxR mate

441 1 P—KB5!   Q—N4
If 1 . . . QxP; 2 BxP mate. If 1
. . . BxP; 2 BxPch, QxB; 3 RxR
mate.
    2 BxPch!   QxB
    3 P—B6   Q—N3
    4 P—B7 dis ch   N—K4
    5 RxN!   PxR
    6 QxPch!   Resigns
If 6 . . . RxQ; 7 P—B8/Qch and
mate next move. If 6 . . . Q—N2;
7 QxRch, BxQ; 8 PxB/Qch, Q—
N1; 9 QxQ mate.

442 1 RxP!   RxR
    2 NxP   Q—K2
    3 NxR   QxN
    4 Q—B4!   R—K2
    5 P—B6!   . . . .
If now 5 . . . R—K3; 6 RxN!,
RxR; 7 P—B7 threatening 8 Q—B6
mate or 8 PxQ/Qch or 8 QxRch,
QxQ; 9 P—B8/Q mate.
    5 . . . .   N—N3
    6 RxR   NxR
    7 P—B7!   Resigns
If 7 . . . Q—KB1; 8 Q—B6ch,
Q—N2; 9 P—B8/Qch and mate
next move.

443 1 Q—K8! K—R4
If 1 . . . RxR; 2 Q—N5 mate.
 2 Q—B6! Resigns
White wins the Black Rook, which
cannot move.

444 1 N—R6ch! PxN
If 1 . . . K—R1; 2 NxPch wins
the Queen.
 2 BxN Resigns
Black is helpless against the coming Q—KN3ch.

445 1 R—K8! Resigns
If 1 . . . QxR; 2 Q—N7 mate.
Meanwhile Black is helpless against
a triple mate threat.

446 1 B—Q6! Resigns
If 1 . . . QxB; 2 NxKBP mate.

447 1 R—K8ch! RxR
If 1 . . . Q—B1; 2 QxBch leads
to mate.
 2 QxBch K—R1
 3 QxRch Q—B1
 4 QxQ mate

448 1 N—Q2! P—Q3
If 1 . . . NxN; 2 R—N5 mate.
 2 NxN! PxR
If 2 . . . NxN; 3 R—K8 mate.
 3 NxN mate

449 1 Q—K5! Resigns
Black must lose the Queen, as
White threatens QxNP mate, and
if 1 . . . QxQ; 2 RxR mate.

450 1 N—R5! PxN
If 1 . . . NxN; 2 QxRPch, K—B1;
3 QxBP mate.
 2 R—KN3 Resigns
There is no good move. If 2 . . .
P—R5; 3 N—K6 dis ch, PxR; 4
Q—N7 mate.
If 2 . . . B—KB1; 3 NxRP dis
ch, N—N5; 4 N—B6 mate.

451 1 RxNch Resigns
If 1 . . . RxR; 2 RxRch followed
by 3 QxR with a piece ahead.
If 1 . . . QxR; 2 RxQch, KxR;
3 QxNch and wins.

452 1 RxN! QxR
 2 Q—B3 Resigns
If 2 . . . Q—B3 or 2 . . . Q—K2
(to stop the threatened 3 Q—B7
mate), then 3 Q—Q5ch forces mate.

453 Black's Rooks are overworked.
He depends on the trap 1 RxB?,
RxR; 2 QxR, QxQ; 3 RxQ, R—
K8ch; 4 N—B1, N—K7ch; 5 K—
R1, RxN mate; but White is too
wily for him:
 1 QxB! Resigns
Black loses at least a piece and
may get mated, for example 1 . . .
RxQ; 2 RxR mate. If 1 . . . QxQ;
2 R/Q1xQ! and if Black captures
either Rook, White mates.

454 1 QxRP! QxQ
If 1 . . . R—B2; 2 QxR! winning
as in the main line.
 2 R—K8ch B—B1
 2 B—Q4ch Q—KN2
 4 RxB mate

455 1 Q—R5ch! RxQ
 2 B—N6 mate

456 1 B—B6! Resigns
White threatens 2 Q—R6 and 3
Q—N7 mate. Black cannot play 1
. . . NxB because of 2 Q—R8 mate.

457 1 . . . . R—Q7!
 2 QxR NxP
 Resigns
Black attacks the Queen and also
threatens . . . QxRP mate.

458 White expects to recover the
Exchange after 1 . . . RxRch; 2
QxR etc. But . . .
 1 . . . . Q—Q2!
 Resigns
If 2 QxQ, RxR mate. If 2 Q—B4,
RxRch; 3 QxR, QxN and Black is
a Rook ahead.

459 1 . . . . NxBch
 Resigns
White's Queen Knight is pinned,
so that after 2 QxN there follows 2
. . . QxRch.

460 1 . . . . R—N3ch
 2 K—R2 Q—Q7ch!
 3 BxQ R—B7ch
 4 Q—N2 RxQ mate

461 1 . . . . N—B6!
 Resigns
If 2 BxN, RxN mate. On other
moves there follows 2 . . . RxNch!;
3 BxR, RxKRP mate.

462 1 ....   R—K7!
     Resigns
Black threatens 2 . . . QxRP mate or 2 . . . Q—N7 mate. If 2 RxR, QxR mate.

463 1 ....   R—K8ch!
     Resigns
If 2 QxR, QxN mate. If 2 NxR, Q—R8 mate.

464 1 ....   P—N5!
    2 PxP   RxN!
    3 PxR   P—N6!
Threatens . . . P—N7 etc.
    4 PxP   P—B6ch!
If now 5 KxP, KxB wins.
    5 PxP   P—R6!
     Resigns
If 6 K—B1, KxB wins.

465 1 ....   RxBch
    2 RxR   QxR
Black has won a piece.

466 1 ....   B—Q4!
    2 Q—Q3   ....
If 2 N—K3, QxN wins a piece.
If 2 Q—K3, BxN; 3 KxB, N—Q4 with the same result.
Or 2 Q—KN3, BxN; 3 KxB, N—R4 again winning a piece.
    2 ....   QxQ
    3 NxQ   BxN
    4 KxB   RxN
     Resigns
Black has won a piece.

467 1 ....   N—B4!
    2 NxN   RxBch
Followed by 3 . . . BxN and Black has won a piece.

468 1 ....   RxN!
Winning a piece, for if 2 QxR, QxP mate.

469 1 ....   Q—K4!
If now 2 QxQ, N—Q6ch and 3 . . . RxR mate.
    2 R—B4   N—Q6ch!
    3 K—N1   ....
Or 3 K—B2, QxQ etc.
    3 ....   QxQ
    4 RxQ   R—B8 mate

470 1 ....   NxP!
    2 PxN   QxNPch
If now 3 Q—KN2, BxNch wins.

471 1 ....   N—K7!
If now 2 NxR Black wins as in the main line. If 2 QxN, QxRch wins.
    2 R/B1xP   RxPch!
    3 PxR   QxBch
    4 P—B3   QxPch
    5 K—R2   B—K4 mate

472 1 ....   R—Q5ch!
    2 QxR   Q—R7!
     Resigns
White has no satisfactory defense against the threat of . . . Q—R7 mate.

473 1 ....   NxBch
    2 QxN   ....
White's Knight at Queen 2 is pinned.
    2 ....   BxNch
Black has won a piece.

474 1 ....   R—QR4!
Also good is 1 . . . B—N6ch! winning at least the Exchange.
    2 R—QR3   ....
If 2 R—Q8ch, B—K1 mate!
    2 ....   B—N6ch!
Because of the pin, Black wins a piece.

475 1 PxP   QxP
If 1 . . . BxP; 2 BxN wins a piece.
    2 NxB   QxN
    3 BxN and wins
White has won a piece.

476 1 B—R6ch   KxB
Or 1 . . . K—N3; 2 PxPch etc.
    2 QxKBP mate

477 1 P—KN4!   B—N3
    2 NxB and wins
White continues 3 QxN with a piece ahead.

478 1 R—K8!   QxR
    2 BxNch   K—N1
    3 Q—R8 mate

479 1 RxP!   R—KR1
If 1 . . . RxR; 2 QxPch leads to
mate.
      2 QxPch!   RxQ
      3 R—N8 mate

480 1 R—R7ch!   KxR
      2 QxPch   Resigns
White's R—KR1ch forces mate.

481 1 RxB!   QxR
      2 BxN and wins
White wins the Queen.

482 1 QxNch!   BxQ
      2 NxP mate

483 1 B—R3!   P—B3
Or 1 . . . QxB; 2 QxR etc.
      2 BxQ   PxQ
      3 BxN/R4 and wins
White is a Rook ahead.

484 1 R—B8ch!   RxR
Forced.
      2 QxQ   . . . .
White has won the Queen for a
Rook.

485 1 R—R4   NxR/R5
If 1 . . . QxQ; 2 R/R5xP mate.
Or 1 . . . P—KR4; 2 RxNP dis ch,
QxQ; 3 RxPch, N—R3; 4 R/R5xN
mate.
      2 QxQ and wins

486 1 Q—KN4ch! Resigns
After 1 . . . QxQ; 2 RxRch and
3 PxQ White is a Rook ahead.

487 1 RxNch!   KxR
If 1 . . . QxR or . . . RxR; 2
QxP mate.
      2 N—N6ch!   PxN
      3 Q—R8ch   K—B2
      4 QxP mate

488 1 RxN!   PxR
      2 BxPch   K—N2
      3 Q—R5   Resigns
There is no good defense to the
threat of 4 Q—R6ch, K—R1; 5
B—N6 dis ch, K—N1; 6 Q—R7
mate or 6 Q—R8 mate.

489 1 R—R7ch   K—R3
      2 RxNch   KxR
      3 QxR   . . . .
White has won a piece.

490 1 N—Q5   Q—Q1
      2 BxN   PxB
      3 NxB   . . . .
White has won a piece.

491 1 QxPch   K—B4
      2 R—B6ch   Resigns
White wins the Queen.

492 1 Q—Q8ch   R—K2
If 1 . . . K—B4; 2 P—N4 mate.
      2 N—Q7ch   Resigns
White wins the Rook.

493 1 RxN   . . . .
Or 1 BxN etc.
      1 . . . .   RxR
      2 BxR   QxB
      3 QxNPch   K—R2
      4 Q—R5ch   K—N2
      5 R—N3ch   K—B3
      6 Q—N5 mate

494 1 NxB   RxN
      2 QxN   Resigns
White has won a piece.

495 1 B—B5   RxRch
      2 QxR   Q—Q3
If 2 . . . QxB; 3 Q—K8 mate.
      3 Q—K8ch   Q—B1
      4 BxPch   Resigns
White wins the Queen.

496 1 NxP!   PxN
      2 P—K7   R—K1
      3 Q—K1!   Q—R3
If 3 . . . QxQ; 4 BxBP mate.
      4 Q—K3!   Q—R5
      5 Q—B4!   Resigns

497 1 NxNP!   PxN
      2 RxPch   K—B2
      3 RxNch   KxR
      4 QxR   . . . .
With two Pawns ahead plus the
attack, White wins easily.

498 1 Q—B7!   Resigns
If 1 . . . QxQ; 2 BxNch wins a
piece. If 1 . . . Q—N3; 2 QxB etc.

499 1 Q—R3!   Q—KB2
If 1 . . . QxQ; 2 BxBch wins a
piece.
      2 BxBch   QxB
      3 QxP   . . . .
White has won a Pawn and has
a winning attack.

500
1 Q—K6ch   K—N2
2 Q—K7ch   Resigns
White wins the Knight.

501
1 R—K1!   Resigns
Black cannot defend himself. If
1 . . . RxR; 2 QxBch, K—K2; 3
QxR and wins. If 1 . . . K—Q2; 2
RxR wins at once.

502
1 QxRP!   Resigns
If 1 . . . RxQ; 2 R—B8 mate.
Black cannot meet the threats of
2 QxR mate or 2 QxP mate or 2
Q—B7 mate.

503
1 B—B8!   BxB
2 RxBch   K—N2
3 KxN   Resigns
White has won a piece.

504
1 BxPch!   QxB
2 R—Q8ch   KxR
3 QxQ   Resigns
White has all the play.

505
1 BxN!   QxQ
2 R—K1ch   B—K2
3 RxBch   K—B1
4 R—Q8 mate

506
1 RxB!   QxR
2 B—N5!   Q—B1
If 2 . . . QxB; 2 B—B6 forces
mate.
3 BxR   QxB
4 B—B6   Q—B1
5 QxQch   KxQ
6 R—Q1   Resigns
Only 6 . . . B—Q2 stops mate,
but then 7 RxB leaves White a
piece ahead.

507
1 R—K7!   QxR
2 QxRch   Resigns
White wins the other Rook as
well.

508
1 N—K6!   NxN
If 1 . . . PxN; 2 Q—B8ch, K—
R2; 3 Q—R6ch, K—N1; 4 R—B8
mate.
2 QxPch   K—R1
3 QxN/K6   Resigns
White can win as he pleases.

509
1 R—K7!   QxR
2 NxB   Q—B1
3 RxPch!   KxR

4 Q—R5ch   Q—R3
5 QxQ mate

510
1 Q—B2ch   Q—N3
If 1 . . . P—N3; 2 R—Q7ch,
K—N1; 3 Q—B4ch forcing mate.
2 R—R8ch   KxR
3 QxQ   Resigns

511
1 RxB!   QxR
2 N—N5   ....
Another way is 2 RxPch, KxR;
3 N—N5ch and 4 NxQ.
2 ....   Q—N3
3 RxPch   QxR
4 N—B7 mate

512
1 BxP   Q—K3
2 B—Q5   Q—N5
If 2 . . . NxB; 3 PxN, Q—N3
(or 3 . . . Q—B4 or 3 . . . QxP
with the same result); 4 NxBch
winning the Queen.
3 QxQ   NxQ
4 NxBch and wins

513
1 K—N3   R—Q5
If the Rook moves on the file, 2
NxB wins a piece.
2 N—B5ch   Resigns
White wins the Rook.

514
1 R—Q6   R—B3
Or 1 . . . R—K2; 2 NxNP and
wins.
2 N—Q7   ....
White wins the Exchange.

515
1 R—Q7!   QxR
2 QxPch   K—R3
3 Q—N7ch   K—R4
4 P—N4ch   K—R5
5 B—Q4   Resigns
White intends 6 B—B2 mate.

516
1 QxRch!   QxQ
2 R—Q7ch   QxR
3 RxQch   ....
And 4 BxN wins a piece.

517
1 BxNP!   Q—N4
If 1 . . . RxB; 2 Q—B8 mate.
If 1 . . . QxB; 2 Q—B6 mate.
2 Q—B7!   P—K4
White threatened 3 BxP mate or
3 QxBP mate.
3 QxRch!   QxQ
4 B—KR4ch   Q—N4
5 BxQ mate

518
1 RxN! QxR
2 NxBch PxN
3 B—B5! Resigns
Black has no adequate defense against the coming 4 QxRP and 5 Q—N7 mate.

519
1 RxN! PxR
2 RxP ....
Threatens 3 N—B5 dis ch.
2 .... K—B2
3 N—N5ch K—B1
4 R—K6! ....
Threatens 5 RxNch.
4 .... Q—R5
5 P—N3! QxRP
6 R—K8ch! Resigns
If 6 . . . KxR; 7 Q—K6ch forcing mate.

520
1 QxB! RxQ
Or 1 . . . QxQ; 2 NxQch, RxN; 3 BxN winning a piece.
2 N—B6ch K—R1
3 NxQ RxN
4 BxN and wins

521
1 R—R8ch! BxR
2 RxBch KxR
3 Q—R6ch K—N1
4 N—B6 mate

522
1 N—N6 R—N1
2 NxB RxN
3 BxN Resigns
White has won a piece.

523
1 .... R—K6!
If now 2 QxR, Q—R8 mate.
2 Q—N2 RxP and wins

524
1 .... RxBch!
2 QxR B—Q6ch!
If now 3 K—B1, B—R6 wins.
3 K—B3 B—N5ch!
Resigns
If 4 QxB, Q—B7 mate.

525
1 .... R—N8ch!
If now 2 K—B2, Q—K8 mate.
2 RxR QxQ
Resigns

526
1 .... B—B7ch!
Resigns

527
1 .... BxN
2 QxB RxPch
3 BxR QxBch
4 K—R1 B—K5ch
Black mates next move.

528
1 .... R—R8ch
Resigns

529
1 .... BxN
2 PxB P—KN4
Black wins a piece.

530
1 .... RxPch!
2 KxR RxR
Black is two Pawns ahead, and will soon win a third.

531
1 .... B—K7!
This wins back the Exchange, leaving White in a hopeless situation with two Pawns down.

532
1 .... RxB!
2 KxR R—K1ch
After 3 K—Q1 (or 3 K—B1), BxN Black has a winning game.

533
1 .... B—R5!
Whichever Bishop White takes, Black replies 2 . . . QxRch and 3 . . . QxB, with a Rook ahead.

534
1 .... N—B5
2 R—B2 NxB
3 RxN RxN
Resigns

535
1 .... Q—Q3!
Threatening . . . QxQ as well as the mate that actually occurs. If 2 QxQ, RxR mate.
2 Q—B3 Q—R7ch
3 K—B1 Q—R8 mate

536
1 .... Q—B5!
If now 2 N—B3, QxQ wins a Rook. If 2 K—B2, RxR; 3 QxR, QxN etc.
2 QxQ RxRch
3 Q—B1 B—Q5ch
4 K—R1 RxQ mate

537
1 .... NxN!
If now 2 NxN, QxRch or 2 KxN, QxN.
2 RxQ BxN
Black comes out a piece ahead.

538
1 .... N—B7ch
Resigns
If 2 QxN, QxN mate.

539
1 .... R—Q8!
2 QxR QxKPch
3 K—N2 N—R5ch!
4 PxN B—R6 mate

540　1 ....　　　　　RxBch
　　　2 KxR　　　　　QxNch
　　　Resigns

541　1 ....　　　　　N—Q5!
　　　2 NxN　　　　　....
　　If the Queen moves, Black wins
　　with ... NxNch.
　　　2 ....　　　　　Q—R7 mate

542　1 ....　　　　　BxN
　　　2 QxQ　　　　　BxQ
　　　Resigns

543　1 ....　　　　　N—B6ch!
　　　2 K—R1　　　　....
　　If 2 NxN, QxQ. If 2 PxN, BxNch
　　wins the Queen.
　　　2 ....　　　　　NxN
　　　3 QxQch　　　　NxQ
　　　Resigns

544　1 ....　　　　　QxN!
　　　2 BxQ　　　　　N—B6ch
　　　3 K—B1　　　　B—N4ch
　　　4 Q—QB4　　　　BxQ mate

545　1 ....　　　　　QxPch!
　　　2 NxQ　　　　　NxBP mate

546　1 ....　　　　　R—N8ch
　　　2 KxR　　　　　QxQ
　　　Resigns

547　1 N—B6!　　　　NxN
　　　2 Q—R7ch!　　　NxQ
　　　3 B—K5 dbl ch K—R3
　　　4 B—N7 mate

548　1 QxR!　　　　　PxQ
　　　2 N—B6ch　　　Resigns
　　After 3 NxQ White is a Rook
　　ahead.

549　1 RxN!　　　　　....
　　Not 1 BxN allowing ... RxP
　　with some chances.
　　　1 ....　　　　　RxB
　　　2 R—KR8ch!　　....
　　White continues 3 P—Q8/Q.

550　1 NxBP!　　　　KxN
　　　2 N—K4ch　　　K—N2
　　　3 R—QB2!　　　Q—R5
　　　4 QxPch　　　　B—N3
　　Or 4 ... K—R1; 5 QxR, RxR;
　　6 QxBch, B—N1; 7 Q—B6 mate.
　　　5 R—B7ch　　　K—N1
　　If 5 ... R—Q2; 6 N—B3 wins.
　　　6 QxBch!　　　PxQ

7 N—B6ch　　　K—R1
8 R—R7 mate

551　1 RxPch!　　　　PxR
　　　2 Q—R5 mate

552　1 B—B6!　　　　QxB
　　　2 KR—K1ch　　B—K2
　　If 2 ... B—K3; 3 Q—Q7 mate.
　　　3 BxNch　　　　K—B1
　　　4 Q—Q8ch!　　BxQ
　　　5 R—K8 mate

553　1 RxB!　　　　　KxR
　　　2 B—K3!　　　Resigns
　　If 2 ... QxB; 3 RxPch, K—Q1;
　　4 QxN and mate follows.

554　1 B—R6!　　　　BxB
　　　2 N/K4xP　　　KR—Q1
　　The threat was 3 Q—R7 mate.
　　　3 R—R8ch!　　BxR
　　　4 Q—R7ch　　　K—B1
　　　5 QxB mate

555　1 R—K5!　　　　....
　　Threatens 2 Q—R5ch, K—N1;
　　3 N—K7ch!, BxN; 4 Q—B7ch and
　　5 R—R5 mate.
　　　1 ....　　　　　R—KB1
　　If 1 ... BxR? 2 Q—R5ch, K—
　　N1; 3 N—K7ch and mate next
　　move.
　　　2 N—K7!　　　Resigns
　　If 2 ... RxQ; 3 R—R5 mate.

556　1 P—Q7　　　　　Q—Q1
　　Else the Pawn queens.
　　　2 Q—Q6ch　　　Resigns
　　White wins a Rook.

557　1 N—K7ch!　　　QxN
　　　2 R—R8ch!　　KxR
　　If 2 ... K—B2; 3 Q—R5ch,
　　P—N3; 4 QxNP mate.
　　　3 Q—R5ch　　　K—N1
　　　4 Q—R7ch　　　K—B2
　　　5 B—N6 mate

558　1 N—N5!　　　　PxN
　　White threatened 2 Q—R7 mate.
　　　2 Q—K6ch　　　....
　　White continues 3 QxR with the
　　Exchange ahead.

559　1 P—K6!　　　　PxP
　　　2 N—K5　　　　Q—K1
　　　3 N—N6ch!　　Resigns
　　If 3 ... PxN; 4 R—R3ch forces
　　mate.

560 1 P—N6! QxNP
If 1 . . . QxB; 2 QxP mate. If
1 . . . PxP! 2 N—N5 wins.
2 BxN! Resigns
If 2 . . . QxB; 3 R—N1 wins
Black's Queen.

561 1 BxPch!' KxB
2 R—R3ch N—R3
3 N—B4! PxP
4 BxN PxB
5 Q—R5 Resigns
Black has no defense.

562 1 N—Q5! PxN
If 1 . . . Q—B2; 2 Q—R8 mate.
2 BxQPch B—K3
3 BxBch QxB
4 RxBch! KxR
5 Q—R7ch K—B3
6 R—R6 mate

563 1 RxB! PxR
2 R—B8! Q—Q4
If 2 . . . RxR; 3 Q—QR1ch wins;
likewise after 2 . . . QxR; 3 Q—
Q4ch etc.
3 Q—QR1ch! P—K4
If 3 . . . RxQ; 4 RxNch forces
mate.
4 BxPch QxB
5 RxNch! K—N2
6 R—B7ch! Resigns
If 6 . . . KxR; 7 NxQch or 6
. . . K—N1; 7 QxRch wins.

564 1 R—K4! P—N4
2 R—R4ch! PxR
3 Q—R6ch Resigns
White mates next move.

565 1 R—K8ch! RxR
2 Q—N4ch! QxQ
3 N—B6 mate

566 1 N—Q5! KPxN
2 RxPch! KxR
3 QxKNPch K—B1
4 R—KB1ch Resigns
White mates soon.

567 1 N—K7ch! QxN
2 QxRPch! KxQ
3 R—R5ch K—N1
4 R—R8 mate

568 If 1 P—N6, QxNP; 2 Q—
B4ch, P—Q4 and Black has a defense. White therefore uses a clearance move to control the important
diagonal:
1 N—K5! PxN
White threatened R—R8 mate.
If 1 . . . QxN; 2 QxQ, PxQ; 3
P—N6 followed by mate.
2 P—N6! QxNP
3 Q—B4ch Resigns
Interposition at King Bishop 2
allows 4 R—R8 mate.

569 1 P—KB4! PxP
2 RxPch! KxR
3 Q—R5ch K—N2
4 Q—R6ch K—N1
5 Q—R8 mate

570 1 P—N5! BxQNP
2 N—K6! P—KR4
White threatened mate in two by
3 Q—B6ch etc.
3 Q—B6ch K—R2
4 B—N4 Resigns
For White plays 5 N—N5ch,
K—R3; 6 B—B8ch followed by
mate.

571 1 N—K5! Q—K3
Or 1 . . . Q—K1; 2 N/R4—N6ch,
PxN; 3 B—B4!, PxB; 4 R—R1ch,
K—N1; 5 QxPch, R—B2; 6 NxNP
and 7 R—R8 mate.
2 B—B4! PxB
3 P—B5! QxN
4 N—N6ch! PxN
5 BPxP QxKNP
6 R—R1ch K—N1
7 QxPch Q—Q4
8 R—R8ch! KxR
9 Q—R4ch K—N1
10 Q—R7 mate

572 1 BxP! RxB
Or 1 . . . QxB; 2 Q—Q8ch and
mate next move.
2 Q—R8 mate

573 1 R—R8ch! KxR
2 R—R1ch K—N1
3 R—R8ch! KxR
4 Q—R1ch K—N1
5 Q—R7 mate

574 1 Q—Q8ch Q—B1
2 RxPch! BxR
3 Q—B6ch Q—N2
If 3 . . . B—N2; 4 R—R1 mate.
4 R—R1! QxQ
5 PxQ . . . .
White mates next move.

575 1 BxP!   P—K3
If 1 . . . NxQ; 2 BxP mate.
     2 B—N5ch   K—K2
If 2 . . . N—Q2; 3 BxNch, QxB;
4 Q—B4 with a piece ahead.
     3 N—N6ch!   RPxN
     4 N—Q5ch!   PxN
     5 Q—K5 mate

576 1 B—N5!   QxQB
     2 Q—KB5ch!   QxQ
     3 RxRch   KxR
     4 R—K8 mate
(Another way is 1 RxRch, KxR;
2 B—N5ch etc.)

577 1 . . . .   N—K7ch
     2 K—R1   QxN!
     3 PxQ   R—R4ch!
     4 PxR   R—R5 mate

578 1 . . . .   K—N2
     Threatens 2 . . . R—R1ch and
3 . . . Q—R6 (or 3 . . . R—R8ch!).
     2 P—K6   R—R1ch
     3 K—N1   Q—K1
     4 P—KN4   R—R8ch!
     5 KxR   Q—R1ch
     6 K—N1   Q—R6
And Black checkmates.

579 1 . . . .   QxR
     2 RxQ   N—Q6ch
After 3 . . . NxQ Black will be
a Rook ahead.

580 1 . . . .   Q—N1!
     2 PxP   B—R6!
     3 PxPch   K—Q2!
     4 QxB   R—R1ch
     5 K—N1   R—R8ch!
     6 KxR   R—R1ch
     7 K—N1   R—R8ch!
     8 KxR   Q—KR1ch
     9 K—N1   Q—R7ch
    10 KxN   Q—R8 mate

581 1 . . . .   P—K6!
     2 PxP   PxP
     3 NxP   N—Q6ch!
     4 PxN   QxPch
     5 K—K2   N—Q5 mate

582 1 . . . .   B—N4!
     2 PxB   N/R4—N6ch
     3 NxN   NxNch
     4 PxN   PxP dis ch
     5 K—N1   R—R8ch!
     6 KxR   R—R1ch

     7 K—N1   B—B4ch!
     8 NxB   R—R8ch!
     9 KxR   Q—R1ch
    10 K—N1   Q—R7 mate

583 1 R—Q5!   Resigns
     If 1 . . . PxR; 2 QxRch and mate
next move. If 1 . . . QxR; 2 Q—B6
mate.

584 1 B—Q6!   Resigns
     If 1 . . . QxQ; 2 R—B8 mate. If
1 . . . RxB; 2 Q—N8ch and mate
follows.

585 1 B—K6ch!   K—N1
     If 1 . . . PxB; 2 Q—Q7ch forces
mate.
     2 N—Q7ch   K—B1
     3 N—B5 d⋮s ch   K—N1
     4 N—R6ch!   PxN
     5 Q—N4 mate

586 1 B—K4!   BxB
     If 1 . . . RxB; 2 P—R3ch, K—
N6; 3 R—B3 mate.
     3 P—R3ch   K—N6
     3 B—K1 mate

587 1 R—B5!   PxR
     2 QxP mate

588 1 R—Q7!   BxR
     2 BxPch!   NxB
     If 2 . . . K—R1; 3 NxP mate.
     3 QxPch   K—R1
     4 N—N6 mate

589 1 N—K4!   BxN
     2 RxB   Resigns
     If 2 . . . PxR; 3 Q—N3 mate.

590 1 P—K7!   NxP
     2 BxN   RxB
     3 QxNPch   K—B1
     4 RxPch   Resigns
     White wins after 4 . . . K—K1;
5 Q—N8ch, K—Q2; 6 B—B5ch
etc.

591 1 N—K6ch!   PxN
     2 Q—B8ch   K—B2
     3 QxNch   K—N1
     4 R—R8ch   B—B1
     5 RxBch   KxR
     6 B—R6ch   . . . .
     White mates next move.

592 1 R—KN3ch   K—B2
     2 QxQch   Resigns

228 · SOLUTIONS ·

593 1 B—Q6!   BxB
      2 N—B6ch!   PxN
      3 R—N1ch   K—R1
      4 QxPch!   KxQ
      5 R—KR5 mate

594 1 B—B7!   QxB
    If 1 . . . RxB; 2 Q—N7ch!, RxQ;
3 RxP mate.
      2 RxPch!   QxR
      3 Q—N7ch   KxP
      4 R—R1 mate

595 1 P—K7!   R—B2
    If 1 . . . QxP; 2 QxQPch, K—R1;
3 KxB and wins.
    If 1 . . . R—B3; 2 P—K8/Qch
winning.
    If 1 . . . KR—K1; 2 RxPch!,
KxR; 3 R—N1ch forcing mate.
      2 RxPch!   KxR
    If 2 . . . RxR; 3 P—K8/Qch
wins.
      3 R—N1ch   . . . .
White forces mate.

596 1 R—QB7!   N—K3
White threatened 2 Q—N7 mate.
      2 RxB and wins

597 1 N—B8!   RxN
    If 1 . . . QxQ; 2 R—N8 mate.
    If 1 . . . QxN; 2 R—N8ch, QxR;
3 Q—KB6ch and mate follows.
      2 R—N8ch!   RxR
      3 QxQch   R—N2
      4 QxR mate

598 1 QxPch!   PxQ
      2 P—B7ch!   QxP
      3 R—R8 mate

599 1 RxN   Q—R5
      2 R—B2   RxN
      3 R—K7!   Resigns
There is no good defense to the
coming 4 QxBch.

600 1 N—K6!   Resigns
Black is helpless against 2 QxB
mate.

601 1 P—R6!   B—B3
      2 PxP   PxP
      3 QxP and wins

602 1 N—B5!   . . . .
Threatens 2 QxP mate.
      1 . . . .   BxN
      2 Q—B6ch   K—N1

      3 QxRch   B—N3
      4 Q—B6   Resigns
White forces mate.

603 1 R—K3!   Resigns
    If 1 . . . BxR; 2 QxNP mate.

604 1 Q—K6!!   BxQ
    If 1 . . . RxQ; 2 N/R4—N6 dis
ch, K—N1; 3 R—R8 mate.
    If 1 . . . NxN; 2 N/R4—N6 dis
ch also leads to mate.
      2 N—B5 dis ch K—N1
      3 N—K7 mate

605 1 R—Q6!   BxR
      2 QxPch   K—R1
    Or 2 . . . K—B1; 3 QxR/B5ch
etc.
      3 QxR/K8ch   R—B1
      4 BxPch!   Resigns
    If 4 . . . BxB; 5 QxRch etc.

606 If 1 P—B6, apparently winning, Black has the resource 1 . . .
Q—B4ch. White blocks off this defense by:
      1 R—K5!   BxR
    If 1 . . . PxR; 2 Q—N7 mate.
      2 P—B6   Resigns
    If 2 . . . BxP; 3 QxBch and
mate next move.

607 1 . . . .   R—N8!
      2 KxR   P—B7
      Resigns
White cannot stop the Pawn
from queening.

608 1 . . . .   B—K6!
    If now 2 BxB, P—R6! 3 P—N3,
Q—B6 forcing mate. If 2 PxB,
QxKNP mate.
      2 QxB   RxQ
      3 PxR   P—R6
      4 R—B2   Q—Q8ch
      5 R—B1   P—R7ch
      Resigns

609 1 . . . .   P—KN4!
Threatens . . . Q—R5 mate.
      2 PxP e. p.   BxB
Black wins easily, as White's
threat is gone.

610 1 . . . .   B—Q3!
      2 RxB   . . . .
    If 2 BxB, P—Q8/Q.
      2 . . . .   P—R7
And Black wins, as one of his
Pawns must queen.

611 1 ....   R—K6!
If now 2 QxR, QxRch and mate next move.
    2 PxR   Q—K7
    3 QxP   ....
If 3 R—Q2, Q—B8 mate.
    3 ....   QxRch
    4 K—B2   Q—B8 mate

612 1 ....   B—Q6ch!
    2 QxB   ....
If 2 K—N2?, QxN mate.
    2 ....   QxRch
Black has won the Exchange.

613 Unable to play . . . QxR or
. . . PxR, Black nevertheless finds a clever interference device:
    1 ....   N—K7ch!
    2 BxN   ....
If 2 RxN, QxR.
    2 ....   QxPch
Followed by 3 . . . PxR and Black has won the Exchange.

614 1 ....   N—B5!
Threatens . . . N—K7ch winning the Queen.
    2 PxN   QxR and wins

615 1 ....   R—Q6!
    2 QxR
If 2 BxR, QxPch; 3 K—N1, Q—N7 mate.
    2 ....   NxQ
    3 BxN   Q—Q3ch
Followed by 4 . . . QxB with an easy win.

616 1 ....   P—B7ch!
If now 2 RxP, BxP!; 3 PxR, R—R8 mate.
    2 QxP   RxP!
    3 QxR   BxP
    4 Q—K2   ....
If 4 Q—R3, QxPch; 5 K—B1, RxB! wins.
    4 ....   B—B5 dis ch
    5 K—B1   BxP
    6 Q—R2   ....
If 6 K—K1, Q—N6ch wins.
    6 ....   BxN and wins
The double pin cripples White.

617 1 ....   N—B6ch!
    2 PxN   QxRch
Black has won the Exchange and will queen his passed Pawn.

618 1 ....   R—N6!
If now 2 PxR, Q—K6ch and mate next move.
    2 QxR   B—R5!
    3 QxB   Q—K6ch
Black mates next move.

619 1 ....   R—B6!
    2 PxR   BxPch
Followed by . . . BxR and Black is a Pawn ahead.

620 1 ....   P—QB4!
If now 2 N—N3 or N—B2, Black plays 2 . . . NxPch and 3 . . . BxN winning the Exchange.
    2 N/Q4—K2   NxQBP
Black has won a Pawn.

621 White, who is ahead in material, expects 1 . . . K—B1 when he wins with 2 R—B4ch!, for if 2 . . . PxR; 3 Q—N7 mate. But Black has a beautiful blocking move:
    1 ....   Q—B2!
    2 BxQch   K—B1!
    Resigns
White cannot stop . . . R—KR8 mate!

622 1 ....   Q—Q3ch
    2 K—R3   N—B5ch
    3 K—N3   N—R4 dbl ch
    4 K—R3   Q—N6ch!
    5 RxQ   N—B5 mate

623 1 ....   P—Q5!
    2 QxQP   QxNP mate

624 1 ....   R—B7!
If now 2 QxR, RxRch and mate next move.
    2 Q—R5   B—B6!
    3 RxR   QxR
    4 Q—Q8ch   K—N2
    5 R—KN1   B—Q5
    6 B—Q6   QxNPch!
    7 RxQ   R—B8ch
    8 R—N1   RxR mate

625 1 B—B4ch!   ....
Not 1 B—N5?, K—B2.
    1 ....   K—R1
If 1 . . . NxB? the Pawn queens.
    2 B—N5!   Resigns
2 B—B7! also wins.

626
  1 QxPch!   PxQ
  2 P—N7ch   K—R2
  3 PxR/Nch   K—R1
  4 R—N8 mate

627
  1 N—K3!   N—Q3
If 1 . . . NxN; 2 R—B8ch wins.
  2 R—B8ch   Resigns
If 2 . . . N/Q3xR; 3 RxR! wins.

628
  1 P—B4!   R—K6
  2 P—B5!   R—K4
  3 R—Q8!   B—R4
  4 P—B6!   BxR
If 4 . . . PxP; 5 BxP mate.
  5 P—B7!   Resigns
Black cannot prevent the Pawn
from queening.

629   White cannot win by 1 NxB because of 1 . . . R—N8ch!; 2 RxR,
QxRch; 3 K—B2, Q—B7ch; 4 K—
N3, Q—N3ch.
  1 QxR!   PxQ
  2 NxB   Resigns
Black is helpless against P—R7
and P—R8/Qch.

630
  1 QxR!   QxQ
  2 P—Q7 dis ch Resigns
White continues 3 P—Q8/Q.

631
  1 P—K8/Qch!   KxQ
  2 B—R4   Resigns

632
  1 P—B5ch!   PxP
  2 PxPch   K—Q3
Forced. Now White can win with
3 B—Q2, but he chooses an even
prettier way:
  3 RxB!   RxR
  4 B—B5ch!   Resigns
If 4 . . . KxB; 5 P—B7 wins.

633
  1 R—Q8ch!   RxR
  2 R—B8ch!   KxR
  3 PxR/Qch   Resigns

634
  1 RxN!   RxR
  2 P—K7   R—N1
  3 R—Q8   Resigns
There follows 4 RxRch, KxR;
5 P—K8/Qch.

635
  1 Q—N5!   QxQ
  2 P—B8/Qch   K—B2
  3 QxNch!   KxQ
  4 N—B7ch and wins
White continues 5 NxQ.

636
  1 R—Q6ch!   RxR
  2 P—N8/Q   Resigns

637
  1 Q—K6ch!   QxQ
  2 PxQ   Resigns
Black cannot stop the Pawn.

638
  1 QxRch!   NxQ
  2 P—Q7   Resigns
White's twofold threat of 3 Px
Nch or 3 P—Q8ch is decisive.

639
  1 N—R5!   PxP
If 1 . . . NxN; 2 PxP wins.
  2 NxN   KxN
  3 P—R7   K—N2
  4 P—B5!   Resigns
Black is helpless against the
Pawns.

640
  1 R—B8ch!   K—R2
If 1 . . . KxR; 2 R—B1ch, K—
N1; 3 P—K7 dis ch wins.
  2 P—K7!   QxP
  3 RxR   Resigns
If 3 . . . QxR; 4 N—B6ch! wins
the Queen.

641
  1 QxRch!   QxQ
  2 P—B7   Resigns
Black is helpless.

642
  1 QxR!   PxQ
  2 P—R6   Resigns
The Pawn marches in.

643
  1 RxB!   RxR
  2 RxR   KxR
If 2 . . . QxR; 3 Q—Q8 mate.
  3 Q—Q7ch!   QxQ
  4 PxQ   Resigns
White queens the Pawn.

644
  1 R—B8!   RxR
  2 R—K8ch!   NxR
  3 P—Q7!   N—Q3
  4 PxQR/Q   NxQ
  5 PxP!   Resigns
The Pawn must queen!

645
  1 Q—R8ch!   KxQ
  2 P—N7ch   K—N1
  3 B—R7ch!   KxB
  4 P—N8/Q mate

646
  1 R—B8ch!   RxR
  2 QxPch!   KxQ
  3 PxR/Nch!   Resigns
White wins easily after 4 NxQ.

647	1 P—R8/Qch	RxQ
	2 N—B5ch	K—N1
	3 RxRch	KxR
	4 Q—R6ch	K—N1
	5 Q—N7 mate	

648 1 RxN!   KxR
Forced.
2 N—B5ch   K—K1
If 2 . . . K—B2; 3 N—K6ch
wins the Rook; likewise after 3
. . . K—Q3; 4 N—N7ch.
3 N—K6!   R—Q8ch
If 3 . . . R—R1; 4 N—B7ch wins.
4 K—R2   R—QR8
5 P—R8/Qch   RxQ
6 N—B7ch   Resigns
White wins the Rook.

649 1 . . . .   P—K5ch!
2 BxP   NxB
3 KxN   P—B7
The Pawn queens.

650 1 . . . .   QxP!
2 RxQ   PxR
Resigns
White cannot stop the Pawn
from queening.

651 1 . . . .   RxP!
2 NxR   Q—B8ch
3 K—R2   P—N8/Q mate

652 1 . . . .   QxRch!
2 QxQ   R—K8ch
Resigns

653 1 . . . .   RxP!
If now 2 RxR, P—N8/Q.
2 R—QN1   K—B6
Resigns
Black wins a Rook with 3 . . .
K—B7 etc.

654 1 . . . .   Q—K2!
2 PxQ   B—N2
Resigns
After 3 QxP, BxQ Black will win
the Rook, remaining the Exchange
and several Pawns ahead.

655 1 . . . .   QxR!
2 QxQ   P—R8/Q
Resigns
Black has won a Rook.

656 1 . . . .   PxB!
2 RxB   QxR

3 R—B1   Q—B7!
Resigns
If 4 RxQ, QPxR followed by 5
. . . R—Q8 and wins.

657 White threatens R—KN8 mate.
If Black tries 1 . . . RxN? then 2
R—QN8ch leads to mate. But Black
underpromotes to win:
1 . . . .   P—B8/Nch!
2 K—N1   N—N6 dis ch
3 RxR   RxRch
4 K—R2   N—B8ch
5 K—R1   N—K6 dis ch
6 R—N1   RxRch
7 KxR   NxP
Resigns

658 1 . . . .   R—R6ch
2 K—B2   RxB!
3 PxR   P—R6
Resigns
The Pawn must queen.

659 1 . . . .   N—N6ch!
2 PxN   PxP dis ch
3 K—N1   N—B7
Threatens mate.
4 RxN   R—R8ch!
5 KxR   PxR
Resigns
The Pawn queens.

660 1 . . . .   R—K8!
2 RxR   NxR
Resigns
The Pawn must queen.

661 1 . . . .   P—Q7!
Resigns
If 2 QxQ, PxR/Q mate. If 2
R—Q1, QxQ wins.

662 White has just played QxQ.
Instead of replying . . . NxQ, Black
nonchalantly advances to queen:
1 . . . .   P—N7!
2 Q—B3   B—N5!
3 QxB   NxQ
Resigns
The Pawn must queen.

663 1 . . . .   B—N7!
Resigns
Black will come out a piece
ahead.

664 1 . . . .   QxPch!
2 KxQ   R—R5ch
3 K—N1   R—R8ch!
4 NxR   PxN/Q mate

665
1 ....   BxP!
2 NxB   P—N6
3 N—B3   ....
If 3 N—B1, P—N7 wins.
3 ....   P—N7
Followed by 4 ... P—R7 and
Black queens a Pawn.

666
1 ....   RxNch!
2 KxR   P—K7
3 R—B1   PxR/Qch
4 KxQ   NxB
Resigns

667
1 R—B8!   RxR
If 1 ... QxQP; 2 Q—B8ch!
forces mate.
2 Q—K7!   P—R3
If 2 ... QxQ; 3 PxR/Qch and
mate next move.
3 QxQ   PxQ
4 PxR/Qch   Resigns

668
1 RxR   QxR
2 Q—R4!   Resigns
Black loses his Rook, as he cannot go in for 2 ... QxQ; 3 R—
N8ch forcing mate.

669
1 QxN!   PxQ
2 RxRch   B—K1
3 BxP!   QxB
4 RxB mate

670
1 B—K6!   PxB
If 1 ... RxR; 2 Q—K8 mate.
If 1 ... BxB; 2 Q—B8ch or Q—
R8ch leads to mate.
2 Q—B8ch   ....
2 Q—R8ch leads to the same result.
2 ....   B—Q1
3 QxBch!   ....
White forces mate.

671
1 QxRch!   KxQ
2 R—K8 mate

672
1 QxP!   RxQ
2 R—B8ch!   BxR
3 R—K8ch   R—B1
4 RxR mate

673
1 Q—B4ch   K—R1
Or 1 ... R—B2; 2 P—Q7, Q—
Q7; 3 QR—Q1 and wins.
2 QxN!   Resigns
If 2 ... PxQ; 3 RxR mate.

674
1 Q—N3ch   ....
Or 1 Q—B4ch with the same
effect.
1 ....   K—R1
2 Q—B7!   Resigns
If 2 ... RxR; 3 QxR mate. If
2 ... RxQ; 3 RxRch leads to
mate. Meanwhile White threatens
3 QxP mate.

675
1 Q—B3!   Q—B4
If 1 ... QxQ; 2 RxR mate.
2 RxRch   QxR
3 QxR   Resigns

676
1 RxP!   NxR
Or 1 ... QxQ; 2 R—K8 mate.
2 Q—B8ch   ....
White mates next move.

677
1 N—B5!   R—Q2
If 1 ... PxN; 2 R—Q8ch leads
to mate.
2 BxR and wins

678
1 QxNch!   RxQ
2 R—Q8ch   R—B1
3 RxR mate

679
1 Q—B7!   Q—N4
If 1 ... QxQ or ... RxQ; 2
RxRch forces mate.
2 P—QR4!   QxRP
3 R—K4!   Q—N4
If 3 ... QxR; 4 RxQ wins. If
3 ... RxR; 4 QxRch forces mate.
If 3 ... RxQ; 4 RxRch forces
mate.
4 QxNP!   Resigns
If 4 ... QxQ; 5 RxRch and
mate next move. Black has no good
move.

680
1 QxB!   PxQ
2 N—B7ch   K—N1
If 2 ... RxN; 3 R—K8ch forcing mate.
3 NxQ and wins

681
1 RxPch!   NxR
2 Q—KB7ch   K—R1
3 Q—B8ch!   RxQ
4 RxR mate

682
1 RxNch!   KxR
2 QxRch!   Resigns
If 2 ... PxQ; 3 R—B8ch and
mate in two more moves.

683
1 N—R6ch   K—R1
2 QxB!   QxQ
3 NxPch!   K—N1
If 3 . . . RxN; 4 R—Q8ch leads
to mate.
4 NxQ and wins

684
1 QxR!   RxQ
2 R—Q8ch   RxR
3 RxR mate

685
1 ....   P—QN4!
2 QxBP   ....
No matter where the Queen
plays, White can no longer prevent
Black's next move.
2 ....   Q—B8ch!
3 RxQ   RxR mate

686
1 ....   P—B6ch!
2 K—N1   QxRch!
3 KxQ   R—Q8 mate

687
1 ....   B—R3!
If now 2 BxB, Q—KB7ch; 3
K—R1, Q—B8ch forcing mate.
2 R—K1   BxBch
3 QxB   R—B8ch!
4 RxR   QxRch and wins

688
1 ....   RxP!
If now 2 QxQ, RxRch with mate
to follow.
2 RxR   RxR!
For if 3 QxR, Q—K8 mate.
3 Q—Q1   QxP and wins

689
1 ....   R—B8!
2 RxR   Q—Q8ch!
3 RxQ   RxR mate

690
1 ....   QxRch!
2 NxR   N—B6ch!
3 QxN   R—K8ch
4 B—B1   RxB mate

691
1 ....   B—KB4!
If now 2 QxB, QxQ; 3 NxQ,
NxBch and mate follows.
2 NxB   QxN!
3 QxQ   NxBch
4 K—R1   R—B8ch
5 Q—N1   RxQ mate

692
1 ....   BxP!
If now 2 QxB or RxB, then 2
. . . Q—B8ch leads to mate.
2 Q—N3   Q—B8ch
3 RxQ   RxR mate

693
1 ....   R—B4!
2 RxR   ....
If 2 RxQ, R—B8 mate. If 2
PxR, Q—Q8 mate.
2 ....   QxQ and wins

694
1 ....   QxNch!
2 RxQ   R—N8ch
3 Q—Q1   RxQch
4 R—B1   B—Q5ch
5 K—R1   RxR mate

695
1 ....   Q—N7!
If now 2 QxQ, R—Q8 mate. If 2
Q—Q3, Q—R8ch! wins.
2 R—Q3   Q—N8ch!
Resigns

696
1 ....   NxP!
If now 2 PxN, QxPch; 3 K—R1,
R—Q8ch! forces mate; while if 3
K—B1, R—Q7; 4 Q—QB5, R—
B7ch; 5 K—N1, RxB dis ch wins.
2 R—K4   QxR!
So that if 3 BxQ, R—Q8ch forces
mate.
3 Q—K2   QxB!
Resigns
If 4 PxQ, R—Q8ch; 5 RxR, Rx
Rch; 6 QxR, NxQ leaving Black a
piece ahead.

697
1 ....   Q—Q3!
Attacking Rook and Knight.
2 RxQ   R—K8ch
3 K—R2   R—KR8 mate

698 White hopes for 1 . . . RxQ?;
2 NxRch, K moves; 3 NxQ winning the King and Pawn ending.
1 ....   QxN!
Resigns
If 2 QxR, Q—K8 mate. If 2 PxQ,
R—Q8ch and mate next move.

699
1 ....   Q—K5!
Resigns
If 2 QxQ, RxRch followed by
mate. If 2 Q—K2, QxQ; 3 RxQ,
RxRch and mate follows.

700
1 ....   N—K5!
Resigns
If 2 QxQ, RxR mate. Or 2 PxN,
RxR mate.

701
1 ....   Q—Q7!
Resigns
If 2 QxQ, R—B8 mate. On other

Queen moves Black can play . . .
QxR.

702
| 1 .... | N—N5! |
| 2 QxQ | R—B8 mate |

703
| 1 Q—R6! | PxQ |
| 2 NxP mate | |

704
1 QxPch!	BxQ
2 R—B7ch	K—Q3
3 N—N5ch	K—Q4
4 P—B4ch	K—K5
5 R—K1 mate	

705
| 1 QxNch! | PxQ |

Or 1 . . . K—N1; 2 N—Q7ch winning.
| 2 B—R6ch | K—N1 |
| 3 NxP mate | |

706
| 1 B—R6! | Resigns |

If 1 . . . QxQ or . . . RxQ; 2 R—B8 mate.

707
| 1 B—R7! | KxB |
| 2 Q—N6ch! | PxQ |

If 2 . . . K—R1; 3 QxRP mate.
| 3 PxPch | K—R1 |
| 4 RxP mate | |

708
1 Q—R6ch!	KxQ
2 N/R4—B5ch	BxN
3 NxBch	K—R4
4 P—KN4ch	KxP
5 R—N3ch	K—R4
6 B—K2 mate	

709
1 R—Q7!	QR—Q1
2 RxB!	RxR
3 Q—B6!	Resigns

If 3 . . . PxQ; 4 R—N4ch, K—R1; 5 BxP mate.

710
1 QxN!	BxQ
2 RxP!	PxR
3 RxP	....

White forces mate.

711
1 QxNPch!	KxQ
2 KR—N1ch	K—B1
3 BxN	Q—R6
4 R—N8ch!	KxR
5 RxQ	....

Followed by 6 R—R8 mate.

712
| 1 Q—R7ch! | K—B1 |

If 1 . . . NxQ; 2 PxNch, K—R1; 3 R—B8 mate.

| 2 Q—R8ch | K—K2 |
| 3 QxPch | Resigns |

White wins the Queen.

713
| 1 Q—R6ch! | K—K2 |

If 1 . . . RxQ; 2 BxRch, K—K2; 3 N—N8 mate!
2 N—N8ch!	RxN
2 B—N5ch	P—B3
4 PxPch	K—B2
5 Q—R7ch	K—B1
6 B—R6ch	....

And White mates.

714
| 1 R—KN5! | RxQ |

If 1 . . . P—N3; 2 N—R6 mate.
If 1 . . . N—N3; 2 QxRch, RxQ; 3 RxRch, B—B1; 4 P—R5, N—R1; 5 RxP mate.
| 2 N—R6ch | K—R1 |
| 3 BxP mate | |

715
| 1 QxNch! | PxQ |
| 2 B—QR6 mate | |

716
| 1 N—B7ch! | QxN |

If 1 . . . K—B1; 2 P—K6, QxN; 3 P—K7ch and wins.
2 BxPch	K—Q2
3 Q—B5ch!	NxQ
4 P—K6 mate	

717
1 QxRPch!	KxQ
2 R—R4ch	K—N1
3 R—K8 mate	

718
1 Q—K8ch!	KxQ
2 N—B6ch	K—Q1
3 N—B7 mate	

719
| 1 QxB! | RxQ |

Or 1 . . . QxR; 2 Q—N7 mate.
| 2 RxQch | PxR |
| 3 RxR and wins | |

White is a Rook ahead.

720
| 1 QxKPch! | PxQ |
| 2 R—K6 mate | |

721
| 1 QxN! | PxQ |
| 2 R—B3 | .... |

Followed by 3 R—R3 mate.

722
1 B—N7ch	K—B2
2 Q—K6ch!	NxQ
3 PxN mate	

723
| 1 Q—N6ch! | K—K2 |

If 1 . . . PxQ; 2 B—N4 mate.
| 2 P—Q6ch | K—B1 |

Other moves are even worse.

3 PxP and wins
Black has no good defense.

724   1 P—B5ch!   PxP
Or 1 ... KxP; 2 Q—B3ch and
White wins as in the main line.
    2 QxPch!   K—N2
If 2 ... KxQ; 3 N—B4 mate.
    3 P—N6   Resigns
Black is helpless against the com-
ing Q—R7ch and Q—B7 mate.

725   1 QxNch!   QxQ
    2 RxP mate

726   1 QxNch!   PxQ
    2 B—B6 mate

727   1 QxRPch!   KxQ
    2 R—R3ch   K—N1
    3 R—R8 mate

728   1 QxN!   NxQ
    2 RxRch   K—N2
    3 N—N4   QxP
    4 B—B3ch   P—B3
    5 BxPch   K—B2
    6 R—KR8   Q—N5
Or 6 ... P—K4; 7 RxPch with
a mating attack.
    7 RxPch   K—N1
    8 R—Q8ch   KxR
    9 R—R8 mate

729   1 Q—Q5!   P—K3
White threatened 2 QxBP mate.
    2 QxKP!   PxQ
    3 BxPch   Q—B2
    4 RxB!   QxB
    5 R—B8 mate

730   1 QxB!   QxQ
    2 N—Q7ch   K—R1
    3 N—QB6 dis ch   N—R3
    4 N—N6 mate

731   1 Q—N5ch!   PxQ
    2 BxP mate
(White has a less showy mate
with 1 B—KN5ch, etc.)

732   1 QxP!   PxQ
If 1 ... Q—K1; 2 Q—R5, N—
K3; 3 KR—B1 White wins quickly.
    2 RxPch   K—N1
    3 RxP dis ch   K—B1
    4 RxQ and wins
White is a Pawn ahead, and
threatens to win a piece with 5
BxN.

733   1 Q—N5!   P—N3
If 1 ... QxQ; 2 RxR mate.
    2 Q—R6!   PxN
    3 R—N4ch!   PxR
    4 BxPch   K—R1
    5 B—N6 dis ch   K—N1
    6 Q—R7ch   K—B1
    7 QxP mate

734   1 N/B4—K5!   NxN
    2 NxN!   BxQ
    3 BxPch   N—Q2
If 3 ... K—Q1; 4 RxBch, K—
B1; 5 B—R6ch, K—N1; 6 N—
B6ch, QxN; 7 B—K5ch, Q—Q3;
8 R—B1! forcing mate.
    4 BxNch   QxB
If 4 ... K—Q1; 5 RxB and
Black is helpless.
    5 NxQ and wins
White has won a Pawn!

735   1 QxPch!   KxQ
    2 PxB dis ch   K—N3
    3 RxBch   K—N3
    4 N—K7 mate

736   1 Q—B7ch!   RxQ
    2 PxR mate

737   1 QxRPch!   KxQ
    2 R—R1ch   B—R6
    3 RxB mate

738   1 Q—R6ch!   KxQ
If 1 ... K—R1; 2 QxRPch!,
KxQ; 3 PxP dbl ch, K—N2; 4
R—R7 mate.
    2 PxP dis ch   K—N4
    3 R—R5ch!   KxR
    4 P—B4 dis ch   NxB
    5 N—B6ch   K—R3
    6 R—R1ch   K—N2
    7 N—K8ch!   RxN
    8 RxPch   K—B3
    9 RxP mate

739   1 QxNPch!   NxQ
    2 RxNch   K—R1
    3 R—N8 dbl ch!   KxR
    4 R—KN1ch   Q—N4
    5 RxQ mate

740   1 Q—N6!   BPxQ
If 1 ... RPxQ; 2 R—R3 mate.
If 1 ... R—N1; 2 QxRPch, KxQ;
3 R—R3 mate.
    2 N/K7xPch   PxN
    3 R—R3 mate

741	1 QxNch!	KxQ
	2 R—Q1ch	K—B1
	3 R—B8ch	Q—K1
	4 RxQch	B—Q1
	5 RxB mate	

742	1 Q—N6ch!	BxQ
	2 N—N5ch!	PxN
	3 PxB mate	

743
1 QxPch!   KxQ
2 NxB dbl ch   K—R3
If 2 . . . K—R1; 3 N—N6 mate.
3 N/K5—N4ch   K—N4
4 P—KR4ch   K—B5
5 P—KN3ch   K—B6
6 B—K2ch   K—N7
7 R—R2ch   K—N8
8 K—Q2 mate

744
1 R—R8ch   K—B2
2 QxNch!   KxQ
3 R/R1—R7 mate

745
1 . . . .   QxR!
2 PxQ   B—B4ch
3 Q—B2   R—R8ch!
4 KxR   BxQ
No matter what White does, there
follows . . . R—QR1 mate.

746
1 . . . .   Q—R8ch!
2 KxQ   B—B6ch!
3 K—N1   R—Q8 mate

747
1 . . . .   BxP!
If now 2 NxQ, N—Q5 mate!
2 B—N2   N—N5 dis ch
3 K—B1   QxN! and wins
Black wins a piece because of the
threat of . . . N—Q6ch.

748
1 . . . .   QxN!
2 BxQ   RxRch
3 K—B2   N—N5ch
4 K—B3   NxRPch
5 K—B2   R—KB8 mate

749
1 . . . .   QxPch!
2 KxQ   N—N5ch
3 K—N1   N—R6ch
4 K—B1   N—R7 mate

750
1 . . . .   QxB!
2 PxQ   R—N3ch
3 K—R1   B—R6
If now 4 R—N1, RxRch; 5 KxR,
R—K8ch and mate next move. Or
4 Q—Q3, P—KB4!; 5 Q—QB4ch,
K—B1! and wins.

4 R—Q1   B—N7ch
5 K—N1   B/N7xP dis ch
6 K—B1   R—N7!
If now 7 QxB, RxRP leads to
mate; or 7 Q—K2, RxQ; 8 P—Q4,
RxRP forcing mate.
7 Q—Q3   RxBPch
8 K—N1   R—N7 dbl ch
9 K moves   R—N8 mate

751
1 . . . .   Q—R6!
2 PxQ   NxP mate

752
1 . . . .   Q—R5ch!
2 KxQ   B—B7ch
4 K—N5   P—R3 mate

753
1 . . . .   Q—B8!
2 RxQ   RxR mate

754
1 . . . .   RxB!
2 NxR   QxRch!
3 QxQ   BxNch
If now 4 K—B1, B—B5ch; 5
B—K2, NxP mate.
4 K—R1 . N—B7ch
Resigns
For after 5 K—N1, N—Q6 dis
ch and 6 . . . NxQ Black remains
a piece ahead.

755
1 . . . .   N—N5!
Resigns
Black threatens . . . QxP mate.
If 2 QxQ, N—B7 mate.

756
1 . . . .   Q—KN6!
Threatens 2 . . . QxRP mate.
2 QxQ   . . . .
If 2 RPxQ, N—K7 mate. If 2
BPxQ, N—K7ch; 3 K—R1, RxR
mate.
2 . . . .   N—K7ch
3 K—R1   NxQch
4 K—N1   N—K7ch
Black is a piece ahead.

757
1 R—R8   RxP
2 R—R7ch   . . . .
White wins the Rook.
(1 R—KN8 also wins.)

758
1 R—R8ch!   K—B2
If 1 . . . KxR; 2 Q—R6ch and
mate next move.
2 RxR   QxN
3 RxPch   Resigns
There might follow 3 . . . N—Q2;
4 QxQch, KxQ; 5 RxN etc.

759
1 RxN!   PxR
2 R—Q1ch   ....
White wins the Queen.

760
1 Q—N6ch   K—K2
2 RxNch!   QxR
3 Q—N7ch   K—Q3
Other King moves lose the Queen
or run into mate.
4 B—B4ch   Resigns

761
1 B—QR3   N—B3
2 N—K7ch!   QxN
3 BxQ and wins

762
1 R—QR1ch   K—N1
2 R—R8ch   K—B2
3 R—R7ch   ....
White wins the Rook.

763
1 Q—R7ch   Q—K2
2 B—B8!   QxQ
3 RxQch   ....
White will be a piece ahead.

764
1 N—K5ch   K—K3
2 Q—KN8ch   Resigns
White wins the Queen.

765
1 QR—QB1!   N/B4—Q2
If 1 . . . N/N1—Q2; 2 NxN,
NxN; 3 R—B8ch winning a Rook;
or 2 . . . KxN; 3 RxN winning a
piece.
2 R—B8ch   K—B2
3 RxR and wins
White has won the Exchange.

766
1 Q—N8ch   K—Q3
2 B—R3ch   K—B3
3 Q—QR8ch   Resigns
White wins the Queen.

767
1 QxRch!   KxQ
Or 1 . . . QxQ; 2 RxB and
White will be a Rook ahead.
2 RxBch   K—B2
3 R—B8ch   K—N3
4 RxQ and wins

768
1 P—B5!   ....
Threatens 2 P—QR3, B—R4; 3
P—QN4 winning a piece.
1 ....   PxP
2 P—QR3   B—R4
3 PxP   ....
If now 3 . . . QxP; 4 P—QN4
wins a piece.
3 ....   P—B3
4 B—Q6 and wins
White wins the Exchange.

769
1 RxPch!   KxR
2 Q—K7ch   K—N3
If 2 . . . K—R3; 3 R—KR8ch.
3 R—KN8ch   K—B4
4 RxNch!   KxR
If 4 . . . PxR; 5 Q—Q7ch.
5 Q—KN7ch   K—B4
If 5 . . . K—R4; 6 Q—KR7ch.
6 Q—Q7ch   Resigns
At last White wins the Queen.

770
1 R—B7!   QxR
2 Q—R7ch   Resigns
White wins the Queen.

771
1 RxB!   PxR
2 BxBP   QxB/Q5
3 QxQ   RxQ
4 BxR and wins
White is a Pawn ahead.

772
1 Q—N7ch!   KxR
If 1 . . . Q—N3; 2 R—KN4ch
wins the Queen.
2 QxRPch   K—N5
4 P—KR3ch   K—B4
4 Q—R7ch and wins
White wins the Queen.

773
1 NxN   QxN
2 B—B3   N—Q4
3 NxN   PxN
4 BxP   ....
White wins the Rook.

774
1 Q—K8ch   K—N4
2 P—B4ch   K—B3
If 2 . . . K—N5; 3 Q—K2 mate.
3 Q—KR8ch   ....
White wins the Queen.

775
1 ....   B—KN5
White cannot play 2 P—B3.
2 Q—Q2   BxR
Black has won the Exchange.

776
1 ....   QxQch
2 KxQ   R—Q8ch
3 K—K2   R—K8ch
Black wins the Rook.

777
1 ....   NxB
2 QxN   B—K3
Black wins the Exchange.

778
1 ....   R—K4ch
If now 2 K—B6?, B—Q2 mate.
2 K—B4   B—K7ch
Black wins the Knight.

779

1	NxP!
2 NxN	BxN
3 RxB	RxP

Threatens . . . R—N8ch and mate next move.

4 N—Q2	RxP

Threatens 5 . . . R—R8ch and 6 . . . R—N7 mate.

5 NxP	R—R8ch

Followed by . . . RxR and Black has won the Exchange.

780

1	Q—R7!

Threatening . . . Q—R8 mate.

2 P—B3	B—B6

Black wins the Exchange.

781

1 B—N6!	BxB

If 1 . . . P—K8/Q; 2 B—R7 mate.

2 KxB	P—K8/Q
3 P—B7 mate	

782

1 NxP!	N—K1

If 1 . . . PxN; 2 QxN!, PxQ; 3 R—KN1ch, K—R1; 4 BxP mate.

2 N—B6ch!	PxN
3 R—KN1ch	K—R1
4 QxPch!	NxQ
5 BxN mate	

783

1 P—N4!	R—R6ch
2 K—B4	R—R5
3 RxB!	PxR
4 KxP	Resigns

Black is helpless against 5 P—N5ch and 6 RxP mate.

784

1 NxB	PxN
2 RxPch!	QxR
3 NxPch	....

White wins the Queen.

785

1 B—R6ch!	KxB
2 Q—Q2ch	Resigns

White wins Black's Queen.

786

1 BxP!	QxB

If 1 . . . R—N1 White replies as in the main line.

2 N—Q5	....

Threatening 3 NxR mate. Black has no good defense.

787

1 K—Q6!	P—Q7
2 K—B7!	P—Q8/Q
3 R—QR6ch!	PxR
4 N—N6ch	K—R1
5 P—N7ch	K—R2
6 P—N8/Q mate	

788

1 R—Q8ch!	Resigns

If 1 . . . RxR; 2 BxQ. If 1 . . . KxR; 2 N—N7ch and 3 NxQ.

789

1 N—N6ch!	Resigns

If 1 . . . RPxN; 2 Q—R8 mate. King moves by Black allow 2 NxQ.

790 Black, though two pieces down, seems to have things all his own way. If 1 K—B1, Q—B7 mate. If 1 K—N2, Q—B7ch; 2 K—R3, Qx RPch; 3 KxN, Q—R4 mate. If 1 N—Q4, RxN with a devastating discovered check to come. But:

1 N—N6!	QxNch
2 Q—Q4ch!	RxQ

Or 2 . . . QxQch; 3 NxQ, RxN; 4 BxN and White remains a piece ahead.

3 RxQ	Resigns

White wins another piece.

791

1 NxRP!	KxN
2 BxN	P—KN3
3 QxPch!	PxQ
4 BxR mate	

792

1 R—N6!	PxR
2 RPxPch	RxP
3 PxRch and wins	

White has a mating attack.

793

1 NxP!	PxN
2 BxB	KxB
3 QxBP	N—B2

Forced.

4 R—B1	R—K2
5 R—B5	Q—N3

Or 5 . . . Q—N5; 6 Q—Q6, R—Q2; 7 Q—K5ch, P—B3; 8 QxN! White gets a decisive material advantage.

6 QxQ	PxQ
7 RxN!	RxR
8 BxR and wins	

White is a Pawn ahead.

794

1 N—B7!	KxN
2 QxPch!	K—N3

If 2 . . . . KxQ; 3 N—N5 mate!

3 P—KN4!	B—K5
4 N—R4 mate	

795

1 B—N5!	QxB
2 RxPch!	KxR
3 Q—R5ch	B—R3
4 QxB mate	

796   1 P—K4!   BxN

If 1 . . . QxP; 2 B—R6!, Qx N/K4; 3 Q—R8 mate. Thus White's first move serves to develop White's Bishop.

     2 B—R6ch   K—K1
     3 PxB   QxP
     4 Q—N8ch   K—Q2
     5 R—Q1ch   Resigns

797   1 BxPch!   KxB
     2 N—K6!   N/Q2—K4

If 2 . . . KxN; 3 Q—Q5ch, K— B3; 4 Q—KB5 mate.

     3 NxQ   Resigns

798   Black is threatening . . . Q— B8ch followed by mate.

     1 R—B8ch!   BxR

If 1 . . . K—B2; 2 Q—B7ch leads to mate.

     2 Q—K8ch   R—B1
     3 RxPch!   KxR

If 3 . . . K—R1; 4 R—R7ch, K—N1; 5 Q—N6 mate.

     4 Q—N6ch   K—R1
     5 Q—R7 mate

799   1 N—QN5!   PxN
     2 N—Q6ch   QxN

If 2 . . . K—K2; 3 RxPch!, NxR; 4 QxNch, K—Q1; 5 Q—K8 mate.

     3 RxQ   Resigns

800   1 R—B7!   R/R6—R1

If 1 . . . R/B1xR; 2 R—N8 followed by R—KB8 mate. If 1 . . . R/R6xR; 2 RxR with the same result.

If 1 . . . R—K1; 2 R—N6! followed by 3 RxQP after Black saves his Bishop.

     2 R/N3—QB3!   RxR
     3 NxR   R—R8
     4 N—K6!   Resigns

He is helpless against 5 R—B8 and 6 R—B8 mate.

801   1 B—KR6ch!   KxB
     2 RxPch   K—N2
     3 QR—R1   R—R1

Despair. He had no good line against the mating threat 4 R—R7ch etc.

     4 RxR   QxR
     5 RxQ   RxR
     6 Q—QN3   ....

White has a winning material advantage.

802   1 N—Q7ch   K—B1
     2 N—N6 dbl ch   K—N1
     3 Q—B8ch!   RxQ
     4 N—Q7 mate

803   1 N—R6ch!   K—R1

If 1 . . . PxN; 2 BxP!, QxB; 3 QxPch, K—R1; 4 QxRch wins.

     2 NxPch   K—N1
     3 Q—N3!   Q—K2
     4 N—R6ch   K—R1
     5 R—B7   Resigns

804   1 K—K3!   Resigns

If 1 . . . P—KR4; 2 N—K4ch, K—B4, 3 N—R4 mate.

805   1 ....   B—Q6!
     2 BxB   ....

If 2 R—Q1, Q—B7ch; 3 K—R1, BxB wins.

     2 ....   Q—K6ch
     3 K—R1   ....

If 3 K—B1, N—R7 mate.

     3 ....   Q—K8ch

And mate follows.

806   1 ....   N—R5!
     2 PxN   ....

If 2 KxN, R—QR8 mate.

     2 ....   RxQ
     Resigns

807   1 ....   BxN!

If now 2 RxQ, R—Q8ch leads to mate.

     2 QxRch   ....

So that if 2 . . . RxQ; 3 RxQ, PxR; 4 PxB with drawing chances.

     2 ....   K—R2!
     Resigns

White's Queen is lost: if 3 R/ B4—B1, Q—R5; 4 P—KR3, RxQ, etc.

808   1 ....   B—QR3!
     2 QxB   Q—Q7

Threatens . . . QxP mate, and also .... BxNch.

     3 N—K2   Q—K6ch
     4 K—R1   Q—B6ch
     5 B—N2   N/K5—B7ch
     6 K—N1   N—R6ch
     7 BxN   Q—B7ch
     8 K—R1   QxP mate

809   1 ....   R—R8ch!
     2 KxR   PxP
     Resigns

Black threatens to mate with . . .

R—KR1ch and he also threatens
. . . PxR/Qch.

310
1	R—B8ch!
2 KxR	R—K8ch!
3 NxR	QxN mate

311
1	N—KN5!
2 BxQ	BxPch
3 RxB	PxRch
4 K—B1	R—R8ch
5 K—K2	RxQ
6 KN—Q2	N—Q5ch!
7 KxR	N—K6ch
8 K—B1	N—K7 mate

312
1	N—B6ch
2 K—B1	Q—N4ch
3 K—N1	N—Q7ch
4 K—B1	N—N6 dbl ch
5 K—N1	Q—B8ch!
6 RxQ	N—Q7 mate

313
| 1 .... | R—R5ch! |
| 2 PxR | P—N5 mate |

314
1	N/Q2xP!
2 PxN	BxPch
3 K—R1	NxPch!
4 PxN	Q—R4ch

And mate next move.

315
| 1 .... | RxP! |
| 2 PxR | BxPch |

If now 3 QxB, NxNch wins the
Queen.

| 3 K—B1 | QxPch! |
| 4 KxQ | B—KR6 mate |

316
| 1 .... | P—KN4! |

If now 2 BxP, NxBP wins. Or if
2 B—K3, Q—B6 (or 2 . . . N—K4)
wins.

2 P—B3	Q—B4ch!
3 K—N2	Q—B7ch
4 K—R3	QxRPch!
5 KxN	RxBch!
6 PxR	Q—R5 mate

317
| 1 .... | B—K6! |

Threatens 2 . . . BxPch! or 2
. . . P—N6!

2 PxB	P—N6
3 R—Q7	P—B7ch
4 K—B1	P—R7
Resigns	

For after 5 K—N2 Black queens
one Pawn and then the other.

318
| 1 .... | N—B6ch! |
| 2 K—R1 | .... |

If 2 PxN, PxP and wins because
of the threat of . . . Q—N5ch.

| 2 .... | N—N5 |
| 3 QxNP | QxBP! |

The Queen cannot be captured,
and meanwhile Black threatens . . .
Q—N8ch!

319 After the promising-looking 1
. . . B—N6 White has 2 RxRch,
RxR; 3 R—QN1! So:

1	P—K4!
2 RxB	RxR
3 PxR	PxB

Threatens . . . R—B8.

| 4 R—QN1 | R—B7ch |
| 5 K—K1 | R—B8ch |

Black queens the Pawn.

320
1	KRxB!
2 RxR	QxP!
3 PxQ	....

Or 3 K—N1, N—B6ch!; 4 PxN,
K—R1 and the threat of . . . R—
N1ch decides.

3	BxPch
4 K—N1	N—B6ch
5 K—R1	B—N7ch!
6 KxB	NxRch

Followed by . . . NxQ with a
winning game.

321
| 1 .... | QxR |
| 2 QxR | Q—R1ch |

Black mates next move.

322
| 1 .... | P—N4! |
| 2 PxP | .... |

If 2 Q—R5, B—N3 wins the
Queen.

2	PxP
3 QxNP	RxR
Resigns	

323
| 1 Q—N3ch! | R—B2 |

If 1 . . . K—R1; 2 N—N6ch
forces mate.

2 NxR	QxN
3 R—K8ch	B—B1
4 B—B4	Resigns

White will be a Rook ahead.

324 Black, who was a piece down,
has just played . . . P—N6ch winning White's Queen. But . . .

| 1 K—K3! | QxQ |
| 2 P—B3! | .... |

Now Black must give back his Queen, for if 2 . . . Q—R4?; 3 N—B6ch wins. White will win the weak King Knight Pawn, with a Pawn to the good.

825
1 PxP!   RxB
2 PxRPch   NxRP
3 QxNch   K—B1
4 Q—R8ch   K—K2
5 QxPch   K—Q2
6 R—Q1ch   K—B1
7 Q—K8ch   K—N2
8 QxKBPch   Resigns
White wins the Rook.

826
1 N—B3!   QxR
2 N—K5!   ....
This move stops the renewed threat of mate, attacks Black's Queen, and also threatens 3 N—Q7 mate.
2 ....   QxB
3 NxQch   Resigns

827 Despite Black's threat to win rapidly with . . . R—R3, White plays:
1 PxN!   BxP
If 1 . . . R—R3; 2 PxPch!, K—N1; 3 N—B6ch, KxP; 4 NxRch, K—B1; 5 QxBch!, KxQ; 6 KR—Q1ch followed by 7 B—B3 and the White King escapes.
2 NxB!   RxQ
3 KRxR!   PxN
4 P—B5!   R—N1
5 QR—N1!   Resigns
Else 6 B—R6 mate.

828
1 Q—R2ch!   BxQ
2 R—N2ch!   KxR
3 RxQ   Resigns

829
1 RxB!   QxR
2 N—N6!   Resigns
If 2 . . . RxQ; 3 NxQ and both Rooks are en prise.

830 Black threatens . . . Q—N8 mate.
1 B—K3!   QxB
On such moves as . . . Q—N5 or . . . Q—Q3 White wins with Q—N4ch.
2 Q—N4ch   Q—K3
If 2 . . . N—Q2; 3 R—QR8 mate. If 2 . . . R—Q2; 3 R—KR8ch and mate follows.

3 QxQch   PxQ
4 RxP mate

831
1 R—K8ch   B—B1
If 1 . . . K—R2; 2 Q—Q3ch wins.
2 RxBch!   KxR
3 N—B5 dis ch   K—N1
4 Q—B8ch!   Resigns
If 4 . . . KxQ; 5 R—Q8 mate.

832
1 R—K4ch!   K—B1
If 1 . . . KxP; 2 N—K5ch wins.
If 1 . . . K—Q2; 2 QxP wins.
2 NxP!   QxN
If 2 . . . QxQ; 3 R—K8ch, RxR; 4 PxR/Q mate.
3 R—K8ch!   RxR
4 QxPch!   KxQ
If 4 . . . K—K2; 5 P—B8/Q dbl ch and mate follows.
5 PxR/Nch!   K—B1
6 NxQ   Resigns

833 In the face of Black's crushing threat of . . . N—B6ch, White finds a clever resource:
1 PxP!   N—B6ch
2 QxN!   PxQ
3 N—B5ch   K—N1!
If 3 . . . K—R1?; 4 P—N7ch, K—N1; 5 N—R6 mate.
4 N—K7ch   K—N2
5 N—B5ch   K—N1
Drawn by perpetual check.

834
1 R—R6!   RxR
2 P—R8/Qch   RxQ
3 P—N5!   Drawn
Black cannot relieve the stalemate position.

835 With a piece down, White manages to find a perpetual check:
1 Q—Q8ch   K—R2
2 R—Q3!   Q—K8
If 2 . . . QxR White has a perpetual check by 3 Q—R5ch etc.
3 R—Q1!   QxR
4 Q—R5ch   Drawn
Black cannot escape from the perpetual check.

836
1 Q—KB2!   Drawn
After 1 . . . QxQ White is stalemated.

837 Black is just about to checkmate.

1 R—B6ch!   PxR
2 QxBPch   K—R2
3 Q—R8ch   Drawn
White has a perpetual check.

838   1 Q—B6!   PxQ
     2 RxR mate

839 White is the Exchange down and he cannot play 1 QxQ because of . . . Q—B4ch and mate next move. Yet he draws:
     1 Q—KN8ch!   KxQ
     2 Q—K8ch!   K—R2
     3 Q—KN8ch!   K—R3
     4 Q—R7ch!   K—N4
     5 Q—R6ch!   Drawn
After 5 . . . KxQ White is stalemated.

840 White's Queen is apparently lost, for if the Queen moves, Black checkmates.
     1 R—N5!   ....
If now 1 . . . QxR; 2 QxRch and wins. And if 1 . . . Q—K3 or . . . Q—B5; 2 Q—N7 mate.
     1 ....   R—K1!
If now 2 RxQ, R—K8 mate.
     2 R—N1!   R—KN1!
Black's best, as he is a piece down.
     3 R—N5!   R—K1!
Drawn by repetition.

841   1 ....   Q—K8ch!
     2 KxR   Q—R5ch
     3 K—B5   Q—R4ch
     4 K—K6   Q—K1ch
     Drawn
White cannot escape the perpetual check.

842 Though Black is a piece ahead, the pressure is troublesome. The simplest way out is:
     1 ....   QxRch!
     2 QxQ   B—N5! and wins
White must either play 3 QxRch or else give up his Queen after . . . R—Q8ch. In either case, Black remains a piece ahead.

843   1 ....   P—K7!
     2 RxP   ....
If 2 R—B2, B—N6 wins the Exchange.
     2 ....   RxR
     3 QxR   NxP and wins

After White's Queen moves, Black plays . . . NxNch with a Pawn up and much the better position.

844   1 ....   RxP!
If now 2 KxR, Q—R2ch; 3 K—N1, R—R1; 4 P—B3, P—N6! forcing mate.
     2 PxP   RxPch
     3 K—B1   RxPch!
If now 4 K—N1, R—N7ch; 5 K—B1, N—K6 dis ch and mate follows.
     4 KxR   Q—B7ch
     5 K—Q3   N—N7 mate

845 White threatens BxR or QxN in addition to QxP mate.
     1 ....   N/Q4—B3!
     2 BxB   ....
If 2 BxR, Q—Q4; 3 P—B3, QxQPch and wins.
     2 ....   RxBP!
     Resigns
Black is well ahead in material, and if 3 RxR, QxQP is crushing.

846   1 ....   RxKRPch!
     2 KxR   Q—K3ch!
     3 QxQ   Drawn
Black is stalemated.

847   1 N—QR4   Resigns

848   1 N—B4   Resigns

849   1 N—K3   Resigns

850   1 RxB!   QxR
     2 N—B3   Resigns
There is nothing to be done against 3 R—N1.

851   1 BxPch   NxB
     2 N—N6   Resigns

852   1 B—KN5!   BxN
     2 Q—Q2!   QxP
     3 B—N5ch   Resigns

853   1 ....   N—R5!
     Resigns

854   1 ....   P—B4
     2 Q—K3   P—B5
     Resigns

855   1 ....   N—Q4
If now 2 QxKP, NxPch.

	2 Q—Q6	NxPch
	3 K—Q2	P—K4!
	Resigns	

856   1 ....   B—N5
Resigns
If 2 N—KN1, P—B6 traps the Bishop.

857   1 ....   P—KN4
2 B—N3   P—KR4
3 N—R2   P—R5
Resigns

858   1 ....   P—KN4!
2 B—N3   P—N5
3 N—N1   BxP
Resigns

859   1 R—B7!   Resigns
After Black's Pawn moves are exhausted, he must move a piece, losing a piece.

860   1 P—R4!   Resigns
After Black's Pawn moves are exhausted, he must play . . . Q—K1 or . . . K—K1. In either event P—N5 thereupon wins a piece.

861   1 R—N5!   Resigns
After Black's Pawn moves are exhausted, he loses his Queen.

862   1 Q—K7ch!   Q—N4
If 1 . . . P—N4; 2 Q—K1ch and mate follows.
2 Q—K4ch!   Q—N5
3 Q—K3!   Resigns
Black cannot avoid mate. Thus, if 3 . . . Q—N4; 4 Q—KR3 mate. Or if 3 . . . P—N4; 4 Q—K1ch forcing mate. And if 3 . . . Q—B4; 4 Q—KN3 mate.

863   1 RxR!   RxR
2 P—KR4!   P—R3
3 K—N2   P—KN4
Hoping to play . . . K—N3.
4 P—R5!   Resigns
Sooner or later the Black King will have to give up protection of the Rook.

864   1 R—R3ch!   PxRch
2 K—B3   P—N5ch
3 K—B4   P—N6
4 PxP mate

865   1 ....   B—B8ch
2 K—N4   P—R4ch
4 K—R4   B—K6!
Resigns
If 4 P—N4, B—B7 mate. If White's Knight moves, then . . . B—N4 mate.

866   1 ....   B—B5!
Now Black can win in many ways, for example:
2 K—N4   K—Q4
3 K—R4   K—B4
Resigns
Black wins the Queen Knight Pawn.

867   1 ....   K—K6!
White is powerless against the following mate pattern.
2 RxP   R—Q8ch
3 R—N1   K—B7!
4 RxR   B—N7 mate

868   1 ....   R—KN1!
2 R—KN1   ....
If 2 P—B6 the Bishop is lost. If the Rook moves anywhere else along the rank, 2 . . . QxBP wins. If 2 R—B2, Q—R8 mate. If 2 BxP, R—N7ch leads to mate.
2 ....   RxR!
3 QxR   Q—Q3ch
Resigns
Black comes out a piece ahead.

869   1 ....   B—R3!
If now 2 BxB, Q—B7; 3 R—KN1, Q—R5ch; 4 K—N2, Q—N6ch! 5 K—B1, Q—B7 mate.
2 Q—B3   B—Q6!
3 P—R4   B—K5!
4 Q—B1   Q—N7!
Resigns
White can do nothing against the maneuver 5 . . . Q—N2 and 6 . . . Q—KR2 mate.

870   1 ....   P—R3!
Resigns
If 1 K—R2, R/B4—B6 wins the Queen. If 1 P—KN4, R/B4—B6; 2 BxR, R—R7 mate. If 1 B—B1, BxN wins. If 1 R—Q1, R—K7 wins.

871   1 P—N4ch!   KxP
If 1 . . . K—N3; 2 R—N7ch, K—R3; 3 R—R1 mate.
2 R—N7ch   K—B6

If 2 ... K—B4; 3 R—N5 mate.
     3 N—K4ch   K—B7
If 3 ... K—B5; 4 R—Q4 mate.
     4 R/N7—N1! Resigns
There follows 5 R/Q1—B1 mate.

872 1 Q—N5ch!   N—Q2
     If 1 ... QxQ or 1 ... N—B3;
2 N—B6 mate.
     2 KR—K1!   ....
Threatens N—B6 mate or N—Q6
mate.
     2 ....   B—N5
     3 N—B6 dbl ch K—B1
     4 NxNch   RxN
     5 Q—K5!   Resigns
He cannot meet the triple mate
threat.

873 1 Q—N4ch   K—Q6
     2 Q—K2ch   K—B7
     3 P—Q3 dis ch! KxB
If 3 ... K—N8; 4 Castles wins.
     4 Castles, mate!

874 1 B—N5!   QxB
     If 1 ... P—QB3; 2 PxP, PxP;
3 BxP, QxB; 4 RxNch wins the
Queen.
     2 QxB   P—KB3
     3 QR—K1!   PxN
     4 RxNch   K—Q1
     5 QxNP   K—B1
     6 Q—N4ch   K—Q1
     7 P—QR4!   Resigns
Black's Queen can no longer stop
mate.

875 1 BxPch!   RxB
     If 1 ... K—B1; 2 N—N6ch
wins the Queen.
     2 RxR   KxR
     3 Castles   P—B4
     4 R—R1ch   K—N1
     5 R—R8ch!   Resigns
After 5 ... KxR; 6 N—N6ch
wins the Queen.

876 1 RxP!   KxR
     2 Q—B6ch   B—Q3
     3 N—N5ch and wins
White regains the sacrificed Rook
with a much superior position.

877 1 RxP!   KxR
     If 1 ... QxR; 2 B—N5 wins the
Queen.
     2 B—N5ch   K—N2

If 2 ... K—K4; 3 B—K7 dis
ch leads to mate.
     3 Q—R6ch   K—N1
     4 R—KB1   R—KB1
     5 B—KB6   QxB
     6 RxQ   Resigns
The threat was 7 RxNch, RPxR;
8 QxP mate.

878 1 R—B7ch!   KxR
     2 Q—K6ch   K—N2
If 2 ... K—B1; 3 R—KB1ch
leads to mate.
     3 Q—K7ch   K—R3
     4 N—B5 mate
Or 4 N—B3 mate.

879 1 QxBch!   NxQ
     2 N—K6 mate

880 1 RxB!   QxR
     2 B—N4ch   K—K1
     3 QxPch!   PxQ
     4 B—N6 mate

881 1 QxPch!   NxQ
     2 BxBP mate

882 1 RxPch!   K—Q2
     If 1 ... PxR; 2 Q—N7ch wins.
     2 RxBch!   KxR
     3 N—B5 dbl ch K—K3
     4 R—K3ch   K—Q2
     5 R—K7ch   Resigns
Mate is unavoidable.

883 1 P—N4ch!   PxP
     2 RPxPch   K—R5
     3 QxRPch!   QxQ
     4 K—R2!   Resigns
There follows 5 B—B2 mate.

884 1 BxBPch!   KxB
     2 Q—N7 mate

885 1 RxBch!   KxR
     2 Q—B8ch   K—K2
     3 NxPch   Resigns
Black must give up his Queen.

886 1 RxB!   PxR
     2 QxP   R—KB1
     3 QxNPch   K—Q2
     4 B—K6 mate

887 1 B—N6ch!   K—B1
     If 1 ... PxB; 2 PxPch, KxP;
3 QxKPch, B—B3; 4 R—N3ch,
K—R2; 5 RxQP and wins.
     2 QxKP   PxB

3 PxP   Resigns
Black cannot meet the double mating threat.

888 1 BxPch!   KxB
2 N—N5ch   K—K1
If 2 . . . K—B3; 3 Q—K6 mate.
3 Q—K6   Resigns
Mate is forced.

889 1 N—B7!   KxN
2 R—KB1ch   K—K1
3 RxBch!   Resigns
Mate is forced.

890 1 Q—R6ch!   NxQ
2 BxN mate
(More pleasing than 1 B—KR6ch etc.)

891 1 QR—Q1!   BxQ
2 R—Q3 mate

892 1 N—N5!   N—R4
White threatened 2 NxBP, KxN; 3 N—N6 dis ch.
2 Q—R5!   P—N3
3 N—B6ch!   NxN
4 BxPch   K—K2
5 B—B5ch   Resigns

893 1 P—B6 dis ch!   PxQ
2 B—K6ch   K—K1
3 P—B7 mate

894 1 NxKBP!   N—B3
If 1 . . . RxN; 2 Q—N6.
2 QxKP!   NxR
3 N—Q6ch   K—Q1
4 B—R5!   Resigns
If 4 . . . QxB; 5 QxR mate.

895 1 NxP!   PxN
If 1 . . . BxN; 2 Q—Q8 mate.
If 1 . . . QxN; 2 R—B8ch! forces mate.
2 R—B8ch!   K—B2
If 2 . . . BxR; 3 Q—Q8ch leads to mate.
3 RxR   PxB
Or 3 . . . KxB; 4 Q—B3ch wins.
4 Q—R5ch   K—K2
5 Q—QB5ch   K—B2
6 RxPch   K—N1
7 Q—K7   Resigns

896 1 RxP!   KxR
2 R—KB1ch   K—N2
3 B—R6ch!   KxB
4 R—B7   Q—Q1

5 RxPch!   KxR
6 QxNP mate

897 1 Q—B7ch!   NxQ
2 PxN mate

898 1 N—K7!   ....
If the Knight is captured, 2 RxNch! leads to mate.
1 ....   Q—B3
2 N—R7ch!   Resigns
If 2 . . . RxN; 3 QxN mate.

899 1 RxBch!   PxR
2 N—Q3ch!   PxN
3 P—KB4 mate

900 1 Q—Q6   Q—Q1
2 R—N8   B—K1
3 RxB!   Resigns
If 3 . . . QxB; 4 Q—B7 mate.

901 1 ....   RxB!
2 QxR   R—R4ch!
3 KxR   Q—R6ch
4 K—N5   P—R3ch
5 K—B4   P—N4ch
6 K—K5   Q—K3 mate

902 1 ....   N—R4!
Threatens . . . N—B5 mate.
2 PxN   Q—B6ch
3 K—R4   B—Q2 mate

903 1 ....   BxQP!
2 PxB   RxP
3 Q—N4   RxBch
4 KxR   B—N5ch
5 K—B1   R—K8ch
6 Q—Q1   Q—QB3ch
And mate next move.

904 1 ....   N—Q5ch
2 K—K3   N/K2—B4 mate

905 1 ....   B—N5ch
2 PxB   Q—K6ch
3 K—B2   NxP mate

906 1 ....   N—Q2
2 BxN   PxB
3 Any   N—N3 mate

907 1 BxRPch!   KxB
2 Q—R5ch   K—N1
3 BxP!   KxB
4 Q—N5ch   K—R1
5 R—Q4   Resigns
He has no good defense to the threat of R—R4ch.

908 1 NxP!   QxN
If 1 . . . PxQ; 2 NxBch, K—R1;
3 RxP dis ch, P—B3; 4 RxP mate.
If 1 . . . PxN; 2 QxRPch! leads
to mate.
  2 Q—R6!   B—Q1
  3 RxN!   Resigns
White forces mate.

909 1 NxQBP!   PxN
  2 R—N8ch! K—K2
  3 QxPch   K—Q2
  4 Q—B8ch   Resigns
White mates in two more moves.

910 1 RxPch!   K—K1
Surprising; but if 1 . . . PxR; 2
Q—R7ch, K—B1 (or 2 . . . K—K3;
3 N—B4 mate); 3 Q—R8ch, K—
K2; 4 R—R7ch and White mates
in three more moves.
  2 R—B8ch   Resigns

911 1 BxPch!   KxB
  2 Q—R5ch   K—N1
  3 QxPch   K—R1
  4 N—B6!   Resigns

912 1 QxP!   Resigns
If 1 . . . PxQ; 2 B—R7 mate.

913 1 BxN!   PxQ
If 1 . . . BxB; 2 QxRP wins
easily without sacrifices.
  2 RxBch   K—B1
If 2 . . . K—R1 White mates on
the move.
  3 R—R7!   Resigns
White has 4 R—R8 mate.

914 1 RxRPch!   KxR
  2 RxPch!   RxR
  3 QxPch   K—R1
  4 QxR   Resigns
If 4 . . . N—N2; 5 P—K6.

915 1 B—KR6!   B—K4
  2 NxB!   BxQ
  3 NxBch   K—R1
  4 B—N7ch!   KxB
  5 NxRch   Resigns

916 1 RxP!   KxR
  2 R—KN1ch K—R2
Or 2 . . . K—R1; 3 NxN, BxN,
4 N—K4!, BxB; 5 QxBch, P—B3;
6 NxKBP winning.
  3 NxNch   BxN
  4 B—K4ch   K—R1

  5 Q—R5   B—N2
  6 RxB!   Resigns
If 6 . . . KxR; 7 N—Q5 dis ch
leads to mate.

917 1 B—B6!   BxB
  2 P—K5   . . . .
Threatens 3 QxRP mate.
  2 . . . .   NxB
  3 PxB   Resigns
He is helpless against Q—N7
mate.

918 1 RxP!   KxR
  2 Q—R5ch   K—N1
  3 BxN   Resigns
Black has no good counter to the
threat of 4 Q—R7 mate.

919 1 NxP!   RxPch
If 1 . . . NxN; 2 RPxP wins
easily.
  2 QxR!   PxQ
  3 NxNch   K—R2
  4 B—Q1!   Resigns
For B—B2 mate follows.

920 1 QxBPch!   PxQ
  2 B—QR6 mate

921 1 B—KB4!   Q—R4
  2 NxPch   K—Q2
  3 B—QN5 mate

922 1 Q—R6!   QxRch
  2 B—B1   Resigns
Black must give up his Queen to
stop Q—N7 mate.

923 1 R—R7ch!   K—B1
If 1 . . . KxR; 2 Q—R4ch, K—
N2; 3 Q—R6 mate.
  2 Q—R8ch!   N—B1
  3 QxNch   Resigns

924 1 NxKBP!   RxN
  2 QxPch   K—B1
  3 BxPch   B—N2
  4 Q—R7!   . . . .
Threatens 5 Q—R8 mate.
  4 . . . .   N—K2
  5 Q—R8ch   N—N1
  6 B—R7   Resigns

925 1 N—K6!   BxN
  2 QxPch!   KxQ
  3 R—R3ch   Resigns
It is mate next move.

926
1 RxB!   PxR
2 Q—N3ch   K—R1
3 B—K7!   Resigns
He is helpless against QBxP
mate.

927
1 NxP!   BxN
2 QxRPch!   KxQ
3 RxR mate

928
1 RxP!   KxR
2 R—R1ch   K—N3
3 Q—N4   B—Q2
Or 3 . . . P—B3; 4 Q—R5ch,
K—B4; 5 N—Q4ch with a mating
attack.
4 P—B5ch!   BxP
5 Q—R5 mate

929
1 RxPch!   KxR
2 Q—R1ch   K—N2
3 B—R6ch   K—B3
4 Q—R4ch   K—K4
5 QxNch   K—B4
6 Q—B4 mate

930
1 RxP!   N—B3
If 1 . . . PxR, 2 QxPch and mate
next move.
2 N—K5   P—B4
3 BxPch!   KxB
4 NxPch!   Resigns
If 4 . . . RxN; 5 QxP mate.

931
1 QxPch!   RxQ
2 R—N8 mate

932
1 RxBch!   BPxR
2 R—B7ch!   KxR
3 QxRPch   K—K3
If 3 . . . K—B1; 4 N—B4 with
mate to follow.
4 QxNPch   K—K4
5 Q—N7ch   KxP
Or 5 . . . K—K3; 6 N—B4 mate.
6 N—B6ch   Resigns
White wins the Queen.

933
1 N—B5ch!   PxN
If 1 . . . K—R1; 2 RxPch!,
KxR; 3 Q—R1ch wins.
2 RxPch!   KxR
3 Q—R5ch   N—R3
If 3 . . . K—N2; 4 P—N6 forces
mate.
4 QxNch   K—N1
5 Q—N6ch   K—R1

6 B—K3   ....
Followed by 7 R—R1 mate.

934
White opens the King Knight
file with telling effect:
1 QxN!   BxN
2 BxB!   PxQ
3 R—KN1ch   K—R1
4 B—KN7ch   K—N1
5 B—KB6disch K—B1
6 R—N2!   R—K2
7 QR—KN1   K—K1
8 B—B6ch!   Resigns
White mates next move.

935
1 R—R7ch!   KxR
2 QxPch   K—R1
3 R—R1ch   Resigns
White mates next move.

936
1 B—B6!   P—KR3
If 1 . . . PxB; 2 R—Q3!, NxB;
3 R—KR3 forces mate. If 1 . . .
NxB; 2 Q—N5, P—KN3; 3 Q—R6
with the same result.
2 Q—N6!   ....
Followed by 3 QxNP mate.

937
1 QxRch!   KxQ
2 P—K7 mate

938
1 RxPch!   KxR
2 Q—R5ch   K—N1
3 B—R6   ....
Threatening 4 Q—N5ch and mate
next move.
3 ....   N—K2
4 P—K6!   NxP
5 R—N3ch!   Resigns
If 5 . . . NxR; 6 Q—N5ch and
7 Q—N7 mate.

939
1 P—R6ch!   K—N1
2 Q—B6   ....
And 3 Q—N7 mate.

940
1 B—B8!   RxB
2 R—R8ch!   KxR
3 QxR/B8ch R—N1
4 Q—B6ch!   R—N2
5 Q—R4ch!   K—N1
6 Q—K8ch   ....
White mates next move!

941
1 RxPch   K—B1
If 1 . . . K—R1; 2 RxRP dbl ch,
K—N1; 3 R—R8 mate.
2 R—N8ch!   KxR
3 R—N1ch   K—B1
4 B—N7ch!   K—N1

5 B—B6 dis ch   K—B1
6 R—N8ch!   KxR
7 Q—N2ch   K—B1
8 Q—N7 mate

942   1 RxP!   ....
If now 1 . . . BxB; 2 QxPch,
B—N2; 3 R—R8ch!, KxR; 4 Q—
R7 mate. Or 2 . . . R—N2; 3 Q—
K6ch forcing mate.
    1 ....   KxR
    2 QxPch   K—N1
    3 R—R1!   Resigns
Because of 4 R—R8ch!

943   1 BxP!   B—B2
If 1 . . . PxB; 2 QxPch, K—R1;
3 N—N6ch winning the Queen.
    2 BxPch   Resigns
If 2 . . . BxB; 3 NxB! winning
the Rook with a discovered check.

944   1 Q—N4ch   Q—N3
If 1 . . . K—R1; 2 Q—N7 mate.
    2 N—K7ch   Resigns
White wins the Queen.

945   1 NxP!   PxN
    2 QxP   ....
If now 2 . . . B—K1; 3 B—Q5ch
wins. Or 2 . . . R—B3; 3 RxR,
PxR; 4 B—Q5ch etc.
    2 ....   P—K3
    3 B—K4!   R—B4
    4 RxR!   PxR
    5 B—Q5ch   Resigns

946   1 BxPch!   KxB
    2 R—B7ch   K—R3
If 2 . . . K—N1; 3 R—N7ch, K—
B1; 4 Q—KB1ch, K—K1; 5 Q—
B7ch followed by mate.
    3 B—K3ch!   RxB
If 3 . . . K—R4; 4 P—N4ch wins
easily.
    4 Q—B6ch   Resigns
White mates quickly.

947   1 RxB!   RxR
    2 QxRPch   R—R2
    3 QxR mate

948   1 Q—R6   Resigns
He is helpless against 2 Q—N7
mate.

949   1 RxP!   KxR
    2 Q—B7ch   K—R3
    3 B—N7ch   K—N4
    4 P—B4ch   K—R4
    5 P—N3   N—R3

6 N—K5 dis ch!   NxQ
7 B—K2ch   B—N5
8 BxB mate

950   1 RxB!   KxR
    2 B—K5ch   K—R3
    3 N—B7ch   K—R4
    4 B—K2ch   K—R5
    5 B—N3ch   K—R6
    6 N—N5 mate

951   1 NxP!   KxN
    2 B—R5ch!   KxB
    3 N—N3ch   K—R5
    4 Q—K4ch   ....
White mates next move.

952   1 RxP!   RxR
    2 RxR   R—B2
If 2 . . . KxR; 3 Q—R5ch and
mate in two more moves.
    3 R—R6   N—B5
    4 RxPch   Resigns
White has won two Pawns and
maintains the attack.

953   1 RxRP!   KxR
    2 R—R1ch   K—N1
    3 R—R8ch   K—B2
    4 Q—B6ch   K—K1
    5 RxRch   K—Q2
    6 Q—N7ch   B—B2
    7 QxB mate

954   1 Q—K8ch!   KxR
If 1 . . . NxQ; 2 R—N8 mate.
    2 Q—B7ch   K—R1
    3 B—KR6   Resigns
Black is helpless against Q—N7
mate.

955   1 P—B6!   PxP
If 1 . . . R/Q2—Q1; 2 QxP mate.
    2 B—R6ch   K—Q1
    3 Q—N8 mate

956   1 RxP!   R—Q2
If 1 . . . PxR; 2 B—R6ch, K—
R1; 3 Q—N5 forces mate. If 1 . . .
NxR; 2 QxPch and mate next
move.
    2 R—R8!   Resigns
If 2 . . . KxR; 3 NxBPch wins
the Queen. Meanwhile White threatens 3 B—R6ch! or 3 Q—R4 with
decisive effect.

957   1 Q—N4!   ....
Not 1 Q—Q4, Q—N4.

1 ....   P—KN3
2 Q—Q4   Resigns
Black cannot stop mate, as 2 . . .
P—KB3 is impossible.

958   1 BxPch!   KxB
2 N—N5ch   K—N1
If 2 . . . BxN; 3 PxB dis ch wins
quickly.
3 Q—R5   BxN
4 PxB   K—B1
5 Q—R8ch   K—K2
6 N—N6ch!   PxN
7 QxP mate

959   1 RxPch!   KxR
After 1 . . . K—B1; 2 R—N5
Black cannot hold out very long.
2 Q—N3ch   K—B2
3 R—R7ch   K—K1
4 Q—QN8ch   K—Q2
5 QxNPch   K—Q1
6 QxRch   K—B1
7 Q—B7 mate

960   1 QxNch!   KxQ
2 B—K5 mate

961   1 RxP!   KxR
2 QxNch   K—B1
3 Q—R6ch   K—Q2
4 B—B6 mate

962   1 NxNP!   PxN
White threatened 2 R—R8 mate.
2 Q—B5   N—B3
3 Q—Q6ch   Q—B2
4 R—R8 mate

963   1 RxP!   BxR
If 1 . . . RxR; 2 Q—N5!, B—
QB4; 3 B—B8! and White forces
mate.
2 Q—N5!   B—B6ch
If 2 . . . BxQ; 3 B—N7 mate.
3 K—N1!   RxR
4 QxBch   ....

964   1 QxRP!   Resigns
If 1 . . . PxQ; 2 B—R7 mate.

965   1 BxP!   PxB
2 QxP   N—Q2
3 N—KN5   Q—B3
4 R—R8ch!   KxR
5 Q—R7 mate

966   1 Q—R5   P—KR3
2 QxN   PxN
3 BxNP   Q—K1

4 B—B6   ....
Followed by 5 QxNP mate.

967   1 R—Q7!   QxR
2 QxP!   ....
Without White's first move, Black
could now save himself with . . .
QxRPch!
2 ....   PxQ
3 B—R7 mate

968   1 NxNP!   KxN
2 Q—K5ch   ....
If now 2 . . . P—B3; 3 NxPch.
K—R1; 4 Q—N3 winning Black's
Queen because of the mate threat.
Or 2 . . . B—B3; 3 N—R5ch, K—
N3; 4 NxB, QxN; 5 Q—N3ch,
K—R4; 6 Q—R3ch, Q—R5; 7 P—
KN4ch winning the Queen.
2 ....   K—N1
3 N—R5   Resigns
If 3 . . . P—B3; 4 Q—N3ch wins.

969   1 QxNPch!   KxQ
Or 1 . . . K—N1; 2 B—B5 and
wins.
2 B—B5ch   K—N4
3 P—KR4 mate

970   1 RxRPch!   PxR
2 N—N5ch   K—N1
3 Q—R6   P—B3
4 NxB   Q—R2
5 QxQch   KxQ
6 NxRch   RxN
7 RxBP   Resigns
White has two extra Pawns with
an easy win.

971   1 Q—R6!   PxQ
2 R—N8 mate

972   1 RxPch!   KxR
2 N—R5ch   K—B1
If 2 . . . K—N3; 3 Q—K3! forces
a quick mate.
If 2 . . . K—R1; 3 NxN, Q—K4;
4 B—N2! is decisive.
3 NxN   NxN
4 QxN   K—K1
5 B—N5ch   Resigns
If 5 . . . K—Q1; 6 Q—R8ch,
K—B2; 7 B—KB4ch wins; or 5
. . . R—Q2; 6 Q—R8ch, K—K2;
7 B—N5ch, K—Q3; 8 B—KB4ch.

973   1 Q—R8ch!   KxR
2 R—K1ch   K—Q3
3 Q—K5 mate

974 1 Q—KR4! R—K1
If 1 . . . PxB; 2 NxP with a
mating attack.
  2 BxRP! PxB
  3 QxP N—N3
  4 N—N5 N—B1
  5 R—K1! P—Q4
If 5 . . . N—K3; 6 N—K4! wins.
  6 BxR QxB
  7 R—K3 B—K3
  8 N—R7! Resigns
There is no defense to the coming R—N3ch.

975 1 QxN! PxQ
  2 RxRch KxR
  3 N—B6ch K—B2
  4 NxQ Resigns
White remains a piece ahead, for
if 4 . . . BxN; 5 BxN.

976 1 RxP! KxR
  2 QxPch K—K1
  3 B—N5! Resigns
White threatens 4 QxB mate, and
3 . . . BxB is impossible because of
4 BxP mate.
If 3 . . . Q—B2; 4 BxPch, K—
Q2; 5 QxBch, K—B1; 6 B—B5ch
winning the Rook.

977 1 NxP! BxP
If 1 . . . PxN; 2 RxPch wins
the Queen.
  2 Q—B3ch! R/B1—B3
If 2 . . . B—K4; 3 N—B3 dis
ch and wins.
  3 N—K4 dis ch! BxR
  4 RxBch K—R1
If 4 . . . K—B1; 5 Q—N4ch
wins.
  5 QxRch! RxQ
  6 R—N8ch! KxR
  7 NxRch K—B1
  8 NxQ Resigns

978 1 RxPch! PxR
  2 QxBPch K—N1
  3 QxN Q—B1
  4 N—K5! Resigns
White has too many threats.

979 1 .... N—B6ch!
  2 PxN Q—R5
  3 R—R1 BxP!
  4 B—Q2 R—B3
  Resigns
White is helpless against 5 . . .
R—N3. If 5 KR—N1, B—B8 mate.

980 1 .... BxP!
If now 2 PxB, Q—K6ch wins the
Queen.
  2 BxN BxBPch
  3 KxB QxPch
  4 K—B1 BxB
  Resigns

981 1 .... B—K6ch!
If now 2 K—R1, R—R7 mate or
. . . B—N7 mate.
  2 RxB R—Q8ch
  3 R—K1 RxR mate

982 1 .... RxRP!
  2 N—B1 R—R8ch!
  3 KxR R—R4ch
  4 K—N1 Q—R5
  5 N—N3 Q—R7ch
  6 K—B1 Q—R8ch!
  7 NxQ RxN mate

983 1 .... N—K7ch!
  2 RxN R—B8ch!
  3 KxR Q—R8ch
  4 K—B2 N—N5 mate

984 1 .... N—B6ch!
If now 2 K—R1, R—R4; 3 P—
R3, BxP and wins.
  2 PxN R—N4ch
  3 K—R1 QxP mate

985 1 .... N—B6ch!
  2 PxN ....
On 2 K—B1, the most effective
is 2 . . . NxPch!
  2 .... R—N4ch
If now 3 K—R1, QxBP leads to
mate.
  3 K—B1 Q—R6ch
  4 K—K2 R—K4 mate

986 1 .... QxPch!
  2 KxQ R—R3ch
  3 K—N3 N—K7ch
  4 K—N4 R—B5ch
  5 K—N5 R—R7!
Threatens . . . P—R3 mate.
  6 QxNch KxQ
  7 N—KB3 P—R3ch
  8 K—N6 K—N1!
Threatens . . . R—B3 mate.
  9 NxR R—B4!
If now 10 P—KN3, R—N4 mate.
  10 PxR N—B5 mate

987 1 .... BxPch!
  2 KxB QxRPch
  3 K—N1 P—N6!

4 P—B3	P—N7
5 K—B2	P—N8/Qch
6 RxQ	Q—R7ch
Resigns	

Black wins the Rook.

988 1 .... BxP!

If now 2 NxP, RxPch!; 3 KxR, Q—Q7ch; 4 K—R3, Q—R3ch followed by mate.

| 2 Q—B3 | P—N4! |

If now 3 R—B8, P—N5 mate.

| 3 P—KN4 | PxN! |

If now 4 R—B8, B—N7 mate.

4 P—N5	B—N2!
5 K—N4	Q—Q4
Resigns	

989 1 .... R—N8ch!

| 2 RxR | Q—QB6ch |

And mate next move.

990 1 .... BxPch!

| 2 QxB | R—N6! |
| 3 QxB | .... |

If 3 QxQ, RxRP mate.

| 3 .... | R—N7 dbl ch |

And mate next move.

991 1 .... Q—B6ch

| 2 B—N3 | P—N4! |

Threatens . . . Q—B8 mate. If now 3 R—Q2, Q—B8ch; 4 R—N2, P—R4; 5 PxP, QxP mate.

| 3 PxP e. p. | K—N4! |

Again threatening . . . Q—B8 mate.

4 R—Q2	P—R4!
5 PxP	Q—B8ch
6 R—N2	Q—B4 mate

992 1 .... R—KR4!

If now 2 P—N3, QxP; 3 B—K4, RxR; 4 RxR, NxB; 5 PxN, BxPch etc.

2 P—KR3	N—N5!
3 BPxN	RxPch
4 K—N1	Q—R7ch
5 K—B1	Q—R8ch

Followed by 6 QxP mate.

993 1 .... QxRPch

| 2 K—N1 | Q—R8ch |
| 3 K—B2 | Q—R7ch |

Black wins the Queen.

994 1 .... RxPch!

2 KxR	Q—R6ch
3 K—B2	Q—R7ch
4 K—B3	R—KB1ch
5 Q—B7	RxQ mate

995 1 .... RxPch!

2 KxR	Q—R6ch
3 K—N1	R—N1ch
4 N—N3	RxNch!
5 PxR	B—KB4ch

And Black wins the Queen.

996 1 .... N—B6ch!

2 PxN	B/N5xP dis ch
3 B—N3	QxBch!
4 PxQ	RxPch
5 K—R2	....

Or 5 B—N2, RxBch followed by . . . R—R7 and . . . R—R8 mate.

5	BxP
6 B—R3	RxBch!
7 KxR	R—R1 mate

997 1 .... N—B6ch!

If now 2 PxN, Q—N4ch or . . . R—N4ch leads to mate.

2 K—R1	Q—R5
3 P—R3	N—K8!
Resigns	

Black attacks the Queen and also threatens 4 . . . QxRPch followed by . . . QxP mate.

998 1 .... NxRP!

If now 2 PxN, QxPch; 3 K—N1, R—N6ch and mate in two more moves.

| 2 PxR | N—B7 dis ch |
| 3 K—N3 | Q—R6ch! |

If now 4 KxN, Q—R7ch wins the Queen.

4 K—B4	Q—R7ch
5 K—K3	N—N5ch!
Resigns	

If 6 K—Q3, N—K4ch wins the Queen. And if 6 PxN, QxQ wins.

999 1 .... Q—N8ch!

| 2 RxQ | N—B7 mate |

1000 1 .... N—B5!

Threatens 2 . . . N—R6 mate. If 2 PxN, BxBP, 3 R—K3, BxPch! forcing mate.

| 2 P—KR4 | QxP! |
| Resigns | |

If 3 PxQ, N—R6 mate.

1001 1 .... Q—B8ch!

| 2 B—N1 | Q—B6ch! |
| 3 BxQ | BxB mate |

This very beautiful combination, played in a blindfold exhibition of 22 games by the great Pillsbury, worthily concludes our collection.

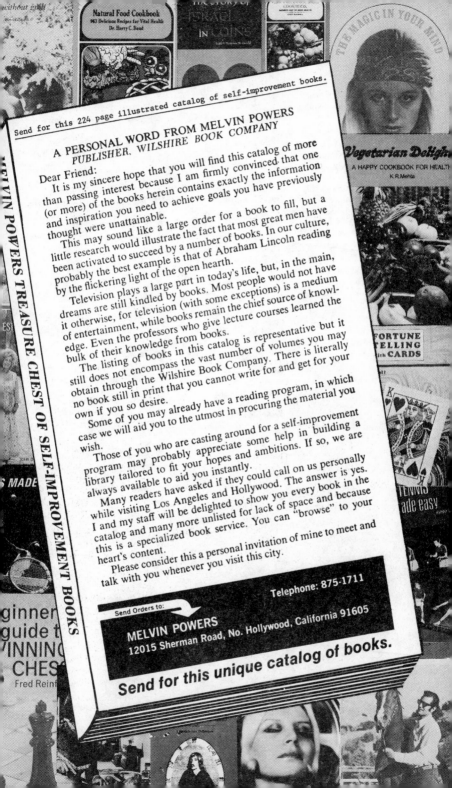

Melvin Powers
SELF-IMPROVEMENT
LIBRARY

____ABILITY TO LOVE *Dr. Allan Fromme*	$2.00
____ACT YOUR WAY TO SUCCESSFUL LIVING *Neil & Margaret Rau*	2.00
____ADVANCED TECHNIQUES OF HYPNOSIS *Melvin Powers*	1.00
____ANIMAL HYPNOSIS *Dr. F. A. Völgyesi*	2.00
____ARCHERY — An Expert's Guide *Don Stamp*	2.00
____ASTROLOGY: A FASCINATING HISTORY *P. Naylor*	2.00
____ASTROLOGY: HOW TO CHART YOUR HOROSCOPE *Max Heindel*	2.00
____ASTROLOGY: YOUR PERSONAL SUN-SIGN GUIDE *Beatrice Ryder*	2.00
____ASTROLOGY FOR EVERYDAY LIVING *Janet Harris*	2.00
____ASTROLOGY GUIDE TO GOOD HEALTH *Alexandra Kayhle*	2.00
____ASTROLOGY MADE EASY *Astarte*	2.00
____ASTROLOGY MADE PRACTICAL *Alexandra Kayhle*	2.00
____ASTROLOGY, ROMANCE, YOU AND THE STARS *Anthony Novell*	2.00
____BEGINNER'S GUIDE TO WINNING CHESS *Fred Reinfeld*	2.00
____BETTER CHESS — How to Play *Fred Reinfeld*	2.00
____BICYCLING FOR FUN AND GOOD HEALTH *Kenneth E. Luther*	2.00
____BOOK OF TALISMANS, AMULETS & ZODIACAL GEMS *William Pavitt*	3.00
____BRIDGE BIDDING MADE EASY *Edwin Kantar*	5.00
____BRIDGE CONVENTIONS *Edwin Kantar*	4.00
____CHECKERS MADE EASY *Tom Wiswell*	2.00
____CHESS IN TEN EASY LESSONS *Larry Evans*	2.00
____CHESS MADE EASY *Milton L. Hanauer*	2.00
____CHESS MASTERY — A New Approach *Fred Reinfeld*	2.00
____CHESS PROBLEMS FOR BEGINNERS *edited by Fred Reinfeld*	2.00
____CHESS SECRETS REVEALED *Fred Reinfeld*	2.00
____CHESS STRATEGY — An Expert's Guide *Fred Reinfeld*	2.00
____CHESS TACTICS FOR BEGINNERS *edited by Fred Reinfeld*	2.00
____CHESS THEORY & PRACTICE *Morry & Mitchell*	2.00
____CHILDBIRTH WITH HYPNOSIS *William S. Kroger, M.D.*	2.00
____COIN COLLECTING FOR BEGINNERS *Burton Hobson & Fred Reinfeld*	2.00
____CONCENTRATION—A Guide to Mental Mastery *Mouni Sadhu*	2.00
____CONVERSATION MADE EASY *Elliot Russell*	1.00
____CULPEPER'S HERBAL REMEDIES *Dr. Nicholas Culpeper*	2.00
____CYBERNETICS WITHIN US *Y. Saparina*	3.00
____DOCTOR PSYCHO-CYBERNETICS *Maxwell Maltz, M.D.*	2.50
____DOG TRAINING MADE EASY & FUN *John W. Kellogg*	2.00
____DREAMS & OMENS REVEALED *Fred Gettings*	2.00
____DR. LINDNER'S SPECIAL WEIGHT CONTROL METHOD	1.00
____DYNAMIC THINKING *Melvin Powers*	1.00
____ENCYCLOPEDIA OF MODERN SEX &	
LOVE TECHNIQUES *R. Macandrew*	2.00
____EXAM SECRET *Dennis B. Jackson*	1.00
____EXTRASENSORY PERCEPTION *Simeon Edmunds*	2.00
____FAST GOURMET COOKBOOK *Poppy Cannon*	2.50
____FORTUNE TELLING WITH CARDS *P. Foli*	2.00
____GAYELORD HAUSER'S NEW GUIDE TO INTELLIGENT REDUCING	3.00
____GOULD'S GOLD & SILVER GUIDE TO COINS *Maurice Gould*	2.00
____GREATEST POWER IN THE UNIVERSE *U. S. Andersen*	4.00

Melvin Powers
SELF-IMPROVEMENT
LIBRARY

_____ GROW RICH WHILE YOU SLEEP Ben Sweetland 2.0
_____ GUIDE TO DEVELOPING YOUR POTENTIAL Herbert A. Otto, Ph.D. 3.0
_____ GUIDE TO HAPPINESS Dr. Maxwell S. Cagan 2.0
_____ GUIDE TO LIVING IN BALANCE Frank S. Caprio, M.D. 2.0
_____ GUIDE TO RATIONAL LIVING Albert Ellis, Ph.D. & R. Harper, Ph.D. 2.0
_____ GUIDE TO SUCCESSFUL MARRIAGE Drs. Albert Ellis & R. Haper 2.0
_____ HANDWRITING ANALYSIS MADE EASY John Marley 2.0
_____ HANDWRITING TELLS Nadya Olyanova 3.0
_____ HARMONICA PLAYING FOR FUN & PROFIT Hal Leighton 2.0
_____ HEALING POWER OF HERBS May Bethel 2.0
_____ HELP YOURSELF TO BETTER SIGHT Margaret Darst Corbett 2.0
_____ HELPING YOURSELF WITH APPLIED PSYCHOLOGY R. Henderson 2.0
_____ HELPING YOURSELF WITH PSYCHIATRY Frank S. Caprio, M.D. 2.0
_____ HERB HANDBOOK Dawn MacLeod 2.0
_____ HERBS FOR COOKING AND HEALING Dr. Donald Law 2.0
_____ HERBS FOR HEALTH How to Grow & Use Them Louise Evans Doole 2.0
_____ HOME GARDEN COOKBOOK Delicious Natural Food Recipes Ken Kraft 3.0
_____ HOW TO ATTRACT GOOD LUCK A. H. Z. Carr 2.0
_____ HOW TO CONTROL YOUR DESTINY Norvell 2.0
_____ HOW TO DEVELOP A BETTER SPEAKING VOICE M. Hellier 2.0
_____ HOW TO DEVELOP A WINNING PERSONALITY Martin Panzer 2.0
_____ HOW TO DEVELOP AN EXCEPTIONAL MEMORY Young and Gibson 2.0
_____ HOW TO IMPROVE YOUR BRIDGE Alfred Sheinwold 2.0
_____ HOW TO IMPROVE YOUR VISION Dr. Robert A. Kraskin 2.0
_____ HOW TO LIVE A RICHER & FULLER LIFE Rabbi Edgar F. Magnin 2.0
_____ HOW TO MAKE A FORTUNE IN REAL ESTATE Albert Winnikoff 3.0
_____ HOW TO MAKE MONEY IN REAL ESTATE Stanley L. McMichael 2.0
_____ HOW TO OVERCOME YOUR FEARS M. P. Leahy, M.D. 2.0
_____ HOW TO RAISE AN EMOTIONALLY HEALTHY,
        HAPPY CHILD Albert Ellis, Ph.D. 2.0
_____ HOW TO SLEEP WITHOUT PILLS Dr. David F. Tracy 1.0
_____ HOW TO SOLVE YOUR SEX PROBLEMS
        WITH SELF-HYPNOSIS Frank S. Caprio, M.D. 2.0
_____ HOW TO STOP SMOKING THRU SELF-HYPNOSIS Leslie M. LeCron 2.0
_____ HOW TO UNDERSTAND YOUR DREAMS Geoffrey A. Dudley 2.0
_____ HOW TO USE AUTO-SUGGESTION EFFECTIVELY John Duckworth 2.0
_____ HOW TO WIN AT CHECKERS Fred Reinfeld 2.0
_____ HOW TO WIN AT POCKET BILLIARDS Edward D. Knuchell 2.0
_____ HOW TO WIN AT POKER Terence Reese & Anthony T. Watkins 2.0
_____ HOW YOU CAN BOWL BETTER USING SELF-HYPNOSIS Jack Heise 2.0
_____ HOW YOU CAN HAVE CONFIDENCE AND POWER Les Giblin 2.0
_____ HOW YOU CAN PLAY BETTER GOLF USING SELF-HYPNOSIS Heise 2.0
_____ HOW YOU CAN STOP SMOKING PERMANENTLY Ernest Caldwell 1.0
_____ HYPNOSIS AND SELF-HYPNOSIS Bernard Hollander, M.D. 2.0
_____ HYPNOTISM Carl Sextus 2.0
_____ HYPNOTISM & PSYCHIC PHENOMENA Simeon Edmunds 2.0
_____ HYPNOTISM MADE EASY Dr. Ralph Winn 2.0
_____ HYPNOTISM MADE PRACTICAL Louis Orton 2.0

Melvin Powers
SELF-IMPROVEMENT
LIBRARY

HYPNOTISM REVEALED *Melvin Powers*		1.00
HYPNOTISM TODAY *Leslie LeCron & Jean Bordeaux, Ph.D.*		2.00
HYPNOTIST'S CASE BOOK *Alex Erskine*		1.00
I WILL *Ben Sweetland*		2.00
ILLUSTRATED YOGA *William Zorn*		2.00
IMPOTENCE & FRIGIDITY *Edwin W. Hirsch, M.D.*		2.00
INCREASE YOUR LEARNING POWER *Geoffrey A. Dudley*		1.00
JUGGLING MADE EASY *Rudolf Dittrich*		1.00
LEFT-HANDED PEOPLE *Michael Barsley*		3.00
LSD – THE AGE OF MIND *Bernard Roseman*		2.00
MAGIC IN YOUR MIND *U. S. Andersen*		2.00
MAGIC MADE EASY *Byron Wels*		2.00
MAGIC OF NUMBERS *Robert Tocquet*		2.00
MAGIC OF THINKING BIG *Dr. David J. Schwartz*		2.00
MAGIC POWER OF YOUR MIND *Walter M. Germain*		2.00
MAGICIAN – His training and work *W. E. Butler*		2.00
MASTER KEYS TO SUCCESS, POPULARITY & PRESTIGE *C. W. Bailey*		2.00
MEDICAL HYPNOSIS HANDBOOK *Drs. Van Pelt, Ambrose, Newbold*		2.00
MEDITATION *Mouni Sadhu*		3.00
MENTAL POWER THRU SLEEP SUGGESTION *Melvin Powers*		1.00
MENTAL TELEPATHY EXPLAINED *Hereward Carrington*		.50
MIND OVER PLATTER *Peter G. Lindner, M.D.*		2.00
MODERN HYPNOSIS *Lesley Kuhn & Salvatore Russo, Ph.D.*		2.00
MODERN ISRAEL *Lily Edelman*		2.00
MODERN NUMEROLOGY *Morris C. Goodman*		2.00
MOTORCYCLING FOR BEGINNERS *I. G. Edmonds*		2.00
MY WORLD OF ASTROLOGY *Sydney Omarr*		2.00
NATURAL FOOD COOKBOOK *Dr. Harry C. Bond*		2.00
NATURE'S MEDICINES *Richard Lucas*		2.00
NEW APPROACHES TO SEX IN MARRIAGE *John E. Eichelaub, M.D.*		2.00
NEW CARBOHYDRATE DIET COUNTER *Patti Lopez-Pereira*		1.00
NEW CONCEPTS OF HYPNOSIS *Bernard C. Gindes, M.D.*		3.00
NUMEROLOGY—ITS FACTS AND SECRETS *Ariel Yvon Taylor*		2.00
1001 BRILLIANT WAYS TO CHECKMATE *Fred Reinfeld*		2.00
1001 WINNING CHESS SACRIFICES & COMBINATIONS *Fred Reinfeld*		2.00
ORIENTAL SECRETS OF GRACEFUL LIVING *Boye De Mente*		1.00
OUR JEWISH HERITAGE *Rabbi Alfred Wolf & Joseph Gaer*		2.00
PALMISTRY MADE EASY *Fred Gettings*		2.00
PALMISTRY MADE PRACTICAL *Elizabeth Daniels Squire*		2.00
PALMISTRY SECRETS REVEALED *Henry Frith*		2.00
PEYOTE STORY *Bernard Roseman*		2.00
PIGEONS: HOW TO RAISE AND TRAIN THEM *William H. Allen, Jr.*		2.00
POST-HYPNOTIC INSTRUCTIONS *Arnold Furst*		2.00
How to give post-hypnotic suggestions for therapeutic purposes.		
PRACTICAL GUIDE TO BETTER CONCENTRATION *Melvin Powers*		2.00
PRACTICAL GUIDE TO PUBLIC SPEAKING *Maurice Forley*		2.00
PRACTICAL GUIDE TO SELF-HYPNOSIS *Melvin Powers*		2.00
PRACTICAL HYPNOTISM *Philip Magonet, M.D.*		1.00

——PRACTICAL YOGA *Ernest Wood* 2.0

——PROPHECY IN OUR TIME *Martin Ebon* 2.5

——PSYCHEDELIC ECSTASY *William Marshall & Gilbert W. Taylor* 2.0

——PSYCHO-CYBERNETICS *Maxwell Maltz, M.D.* 2.0

——PSYCHOLOGY OF HANDWRITING *Nadya Olyanova* 2.0

——PSYCHOSOMATIC GYNECOLOGY *William S. Kroger, M.D.* 10.0

——ROMANCE OF HASSIDISM *Jacob S. Minkin* 2.5

——SECRET OF BOWLING STRIKES *Dawson Taylor* 2.0

——SECRET OF PERFECT PUTTING *Horton Smith & Dawson Taylor* 2.0

——SECRET OF SECRETS *U. S. Andersen* 2.0

——SECRETS OF HYPNOTISM *S. J. Van Pelt, M.D.* 2.0

——SEEING INTO THE FUTURE *Harvey Day* 2.0

——SELF-CONFIDENCE THROUGH SELF-ANALYSIS *E. Oakley* 1.0

——SELF-HYPNOSIS *Paul Adams* 2.0

——SELF-HYPNOSIS Its Theory, Technique & Application *Melvin Powers* 2.0

——SELF-HYPNOSIS A Conditioned-Response Technique *Laurance Sparks* 2.0

——SERVICE OF THE HEART *Evelyn Garfield, Ph.D.* 2.5

——7 DAYS TO FASTER READING *William S. Schaill* 2.0

——SEW SIMPLY, SEW RIGHT *Mini Rhea & F. Leighton* 2.0

——SEX AND HYPNOSIS *L. T. Woodward, M.D.* 2.0

——SEX WITHOUT GUILT *Albert Ellis, Ph.D.* 2.0

——SEXUALLY ADEQUATE FEMALE *Frank S. Caprio, M.D.* 2.0

——SEXUALLY ADEQUATE MALE *Frank S. Caprio, M.D.* 2.0

——STAMP COLLECTING FOR BEGINNERS *Burton Hobson* 2.0

——STAMP COLLECTING FOR FUN & PROFIT *Frank Cetin* 1.0

——STORY OF ISRAEL IN COINS *Jean & Maurice Gould* 2.0

——STORY OF ISRAEL IN STAMPS *Maxim & Gabriel Shamir* 1.0

——STUDENT'S GUIDE TO BETTER GRADES *J. A. Rickard* 2.0

——STUDENT'S GUIDE TO EFFICIENT STUDY *D. E. James* 1.0

——STUTTERING AND WHAT YOU CAN DO ABOUT IT *W. Johnson, Ph.D.* 2.0

——SUCCESS-CYBERNETICS *U. S. Andersen* 2.0

——TABLE TENNIS MADE EASY *Johnny Leach* 2.0

——TAROT *Mouni Sadhu* 3.0

——TAROT OF THE BOHEMIANS *Papus* 3.0

——10 DAYS TO A GREAT NEW LIFE *William E. Edwards* 2.0

——TENNIS MADE EASY *Joel Brecheen* 2.0

——TEST YOUR ESP *Martin Ebon* 2.0

——THERAPY THROUGH HYPNOSIS *edited by Raphael H. Rhodes* 3.0

——THINK AND GROW RICH *Napoleon Hill* 2.0

——THOUGHT DIAL *Sydney Omarr* 2.0

——THREE MAGIC WORDS *U. S. Andersen* 2.0

——TONGUE OF THE PROPHETS *Robert St. John* 3.0

——TREASURY OF COMFORT *edited by Rabbi Sidney Greenberg* 2.0

——TREASURY OF THE ART OF LIVING *edited by Rabbi S. Greenberg* 2.0

——VEGETABLE GARDENING FOR BEGINNERS *Hugh Wiberg* 2.0

——VEGETABLES FOR TODAY'S GARDENS *R. Milton Carleton* 2.0

——VEGETARIAN COOKERY *Janet Walker* 2.0

——VEGETARIAN COOKING MADE EASY & DELECTABLE *Veronica Vezza* 2.0

——VEGETARIAN DELIGHTS — A Happy Cookbook for Health *K. R. Mehta* 2.0

——VEGETARIAN GOURMET COOKBOOK *Joyce McKinnel* 2.0

——WITCHCRAFT, MAGIC & OCCULTISM—A Fascinating History *W. B. Crow* 3.0

——WITCHCRAFT—THE SIX SENSE *Justine Glass* 2.0

——YOU ARE NOT THE TARGET *Laura Huxley* 2.0

——YOU CAN ANALYZE HANDWRITING *Robert Holder* 2.0

——YOU CAN LEARN TO RELAX *Dr. Samuel Gutwirth* 2.0

——YOUR SUBCONSCIOUS POWER *Charles M. Simmons* 2.0

——YOUR THOUGHTS CAN CHANGE YOUR LIFE *Donald Curtis* 2.0

——YOUR WILL & WHAT TO DO ABOUT IT *Attorney Samuel G. Kling* 2.0

——ZODIAC REVEALED *Rupert Gleadow* 2.0

WILSHIRE
HORSE LOVERS'
LIBRARY

AMATEUR HORSE BREEDER A. C. Leighton Hardman	2.00
AMERICAN QUARTER HORSE IN PICTURES Margaret Cabell Self	2.00
APPALOOSA HORSE Bill & Dona Richardson	2.00
ARABIAN HORSE Reginald S. Summerhays	2.00
AT THE HORSE SHOW Margaret Cabell Self	2.00
BACK-YARD FOAL Peggy Jett Pittinger	2.00
BACK-YARD HORSE Peggy Jett Pittinger	2.00
BASIC DRESSAGE Jean Froissard	2.00
BITS—THEIR HISTORY, USE AND MISUSE Louis Taylor	2.00
CAVALRY MANUAL OF HORSEMANSHIP Gordon Wright	2.00
COMPLETE TRAINING OF HORSE AND RIDER Colonel Alois Podhajsky	3.00
DRESSAGE—A study of the Finer Points in Riding Henry Wynmalen	3.00
DRIVING HORSES Sallie Walrond	2.00
EQUITATION Jean Froissard	3.00
FIRST AID FOR HORSES Dr. Charles H. Denning, Jr.	2.00
FUN OF RAISING A COLT Rubye & Frank Griffith	2.00
FUN ON HORSEBACK Margaret Cabell Self	2.00
HORSE OWNER'S CONCISE GUIDE Elsie V. Hanauer	2.00
HORSE SELECTION & CARE FOR BEGINNERS George H. Conn	2.00
HORSE SENSE—A complete guide to riding and care Alan Deacon	4.00
HORSEBACK RIDING FOR BEGINNERS Louis Taylor	3.00
HORSEBACK RIDING MADE EASY & FUN Sue Henderson Coen	2.00
HORSES—Their Selection, Care & Handling Margaret Cabell Self	2.00
ILLUSTRATED BOOK OF THE HORSE S. Sidney (8½" x 11½")	10.00
ILLUSTRATED HORSE MANAGEMENT—400 Illustrations Dr. E. Mayhew	5.00
ILLUSTRATED HORSE TRAINING Captain M. H. Hayes	5.00
ILLUSTRATED HORSEBACK RIDING FOR BEGINNERS Jeanne Mellin	2.00
JUMPING—Learning and Teaching Jean Froissard	2.00
LIPIZZANERS AND THE SPANISH RIDING SCHOOL W. Reuter	2.00
MORGAN HORSE IN PICTURES Margaret Cabell Self	2.00
POLICE HORSES Judith Campbell	2.00
PRACTICAL GUIDE TO HORSESHOEING	2.00
PROBLEM HORSES Reginald S. Summerhays	
Tested Guide for Curing Most Common & Serious Horse Behavior Habits	2.00
RESCHOOLING THE THOROUGHBRED Peggy Jett Pittenger	2.00
SCHOOLING YOUR YOUNG HORSE George Wheatley	2.00
TEACHING YOUR HORSE TO JUMP W. J. Froud	2.00
THE LAW AND YOUR HORSE Edward H. Greene	3.00
TRAIL HORSES & TRAIL RIDING Anne & Perry Westbrook	2.00
TREATING HORSE AILMENTS G. W. Serth	2.00
WONDERFUL WORLD OF PONIES Peggy Jett Pittenger (8½" x 11½")	4.00
YOUR PONY BOOK Hermann Wiederhold	2.00
YOUR WESTERN HORSE Nelson C. Nye	2.00

Books of Special Interest

DOG TRAINING MADE EASY & FUN John W. Kellogg	2.00
PIGEONS: HOW TO RAISE AND TRAIN THEM William H. Allen, Jr.	2.00

*The books listed above can be obtained from your book dealer or directly from
Wilshire Book Company. When ordering, please remit 10c per book postage.
Send for our free 224 page illustrated catalog of self-improvement books.*

Wilshire Book Company
12015 Sherman Road, No. Hollywood, California 91605

Notes